The Phoenicians

The Phoenicians

Text by **Aldo Massa**

Translated by David Macrae

Minerva

Contents

Alinari 5, 10, 11, 30 — Archives 25, 38, 119, 125 —
Boyer 56b) — Fiore 13, 15b), 27a), 40, 127a), 127b) —
Pfaltzer 29a), 29b), 41, 44, 78b), 79, 97 — Roger-
Viollet 2, 7, 8, 9, 16, 19, 20, 24, 28, 32, 43, 46, 49,
50, 52, 54, 55, 58, 60, 63, 64, 66, 68, 72, 74, 77b),
80, 82, 84, 86, 92, 95, 98, 101, 104, 107, 110, 111b),
112, 114, 117, 122, 128, 131, 132, 133, 134, 142,
144 — SEF 14, 15a), 17, 31, 35, 53, 56a), 71, 73, 91,
103, 109, 120, 137, 137, 140.

© Editions Minerva S.A., Genève, 1977
Printer, industria gráfica sa
Tuset, 19 Barcelona   Sant Vicenç dels Horts 1977
Depósito legal B. 8951-1977
Printed in Spain

1 The Phoenician crucible

Between the sea and the steep foothills of the great Lebanese peaks there is only room for a more or less cramped beach; and even that is interrupted by towering rocky headlands. For centuries, before man had learnt how to overcome the steep grades by engineering techniques, it was difficult, and at times impossible, to follow the coast, at least by land. During the heavy autumnal rains and the spring thaw, the fords at the river mouths were impassable, as the gushing torrents of water would have swept any boat to certain doom. Even if the traveller had succeeded in getting across, he would still have been confronted by one of those mighty spurs of rock which reached down from the mountain ranges inland to the sea, where they presented a formidable barrier. Man's use of iron later enabled him to dig paths, or rather steps, into these rugged cliffs.

The term *Phoenicians* is used to denote the tribes which settled on the coast, at the foot of Lebanon, at least 2,000 years before the birth of Christ, while other related peoples occupied the hinterland, north and south. The Greeks offered a number of etymologies for this name, deriving it from the name of the palm-tree

Phoenician goddess—statuette found in Lebanon (1000 BC).

and also from the color red, which was a favorite of the people which, for many years, had a monopoly over the manufacture of purple. Nowadays it is agreed that the word *Phoenician* is a corruption of the name used by the Egyptians to designate the entire group of peoples which inhabited Arabia and the Persian Gulf, an area known to them as *Poun-t.* The original root has been much better preserved in forms such as *Poeni, Punici,* whereby the Latin language referred to the Phoenicians of Africa, with whom Rome had such persistent trouble.

What route had the Phoenicians followed to reach Syria, and where had they come from? According to a tradition which Herodotus heard directly from their descendants, before settling on the Syrian coast, they had lived on the shores of the Persian Gulf. During that first phase of their collective existence, which they still remembered, they had lived on the Bahrein group of islands; in the time of Strabo, two of those islands were still called Tyr and Arados. They were understood to be the metropolis of the great Syrian cities to which these names owe their fame; apparently they

contained temples which were virtually indistinguishable from Phoenician temples. It is possible that some of these resemblances and patterns of similarity between the Phoenicia of the Indian Ocean and that of the Mediterranean are attributable to the island-dwellers of the Persian Gulf, who, at some quite late stage, saw this as a means of attracting visitors anxious to see the cradle of a people which had played such a prominent role in the ancient world. However, the substance of this account must be true, as both Hebrew and Greek sources record the fact of great migrations which, about the time of the first Theban Empire, had brought to Syria peoples known as the Canaanites, of which the Phoenicians were the eastern branch.

In order to reach their new home the migrants might have crossed the north Arabian deserts, following a line of oases; alternatively, they might have gone up the Euphrates Valley, from south to north, crossed the fords on this river, and then swung around towards the south and south-west. Opinions are divided on this subject; it is certain, however, that the newcomers seized the territory from the semi-barbar-

6

ian tribes which had occupied it hitherto. From Aleppo and Damascus to the Nile and the Sinai Peninsula, the newcomers settled in the areas that they found most suitable for their needs; while some of them moved into northern Egypt and founded a dominant pastoral civilization which lasted several centuries, others occupied the entire coastline from Mount Carmel to Mount Casius, where they founded cities which, thanks to the outstanding natural defences provided by a backdrop of sheer mountains, were destined for a brilliant future. It was the latter group which became the Phoenicians of history.

Which family of peoples did the Phoenicians belong to? On the basis of the genealogical table found in Chapter X of the Book of Genesis,

they have been regarded as members of what is known as the Kush race. This would make them, and all the Canaanites, the cousins of the Egyptians, who, according to that same genealogy, are also the sons of Cham. On the other hand, ever since the deciphering of the Phoenician inscriptions, it has been evident—though it came as no surprise—that Phoenician and Hebrew are very similar. In fact, they are virtually two dialects of the same language. A case could surely be made, therefore, for relating the Phoenicians to that great Semitic race of which the Hebrews are the most illustrious representatives, though the exact degree of relationship would be open to some debate. In any case, the Phoenicians were probably closer kin to the Hebrews than to the Egyptians and the other peoples known by the name of Kush or Cham. Differences of environment and destiny eventually accounted for that difference of religion which authors so emphasize when attributing to the two nations a separate origin.

8

Left: view of the peaks of Anti Lebanon, not far from Baalbek. Above: the Djebel Mouskiye mountains.

Without a doubt customs and, later on, beliefs, were not the same in Jerusalem as in Sidon and Tyr; but no argument based on these dissimilarities could lessen the weight of an identical language. If one accepts the hypothesis of a Kush origin for the Phoenicians this identity of language can be explained in one way only: it would be necessary to admit that the Hebrews had influenced the Phoenicians so strongly that they borrowed and adopted the language of Abraham. However, such a hypothesis would pose many problems, and also run directly counter to everything we know about the history of the area.

It was not until David and Solomon that the Hebrews won for themselves an imposing political and military dominion in Syria. Yet, while the Jewish empire was beginning to play this dominant but short-lived role, from Damascus to the Red Sea, Phoenicia had already existed for several centuries. Moreover, we have no reason to believe that, well before that time, it did not have its own language and script.

9

Early Phoenician statuettes (Ugarit).

Moreover, as can be surmised from works of history and prophecy, it was most certainly Phoenicia which influenced the Hebrew people, rather than the other way around, throughout this entire period, even during the reigns of the kings of Juda and Israel, as well as before and after the schism of the ten tribes.

It does not seem that the Jews, from the time of David to the captivity, ever tried to subdue Phoenicia or bring it under their control in any way; neither do they seem to have given it any of their ideas or customs. In fact, they sent to Tyr for the architect and craftsmen who built and decorated the temple of Jehovah. Despite the prophets they never ceased to borrow from that same people their gods and the relevant modes of worship, as well as the images and symbols with which they were represented. A Tyrian princess, Athalia, reigned in Jerusalem, whereas there are no grounds whatever for assuming that a Jew ever enjoyed the same kind of good fortune in the coastal cities. Unless it be at the time of the royalty, one wonders exactly when the Jews achieved such distinct sway over their rich and industrious neighbors as to cause

them to abandon the language—certainly non-Semitic—which they had brought with them from their distant home. When precisely did the substitution take place?

If one were to study the whole of the history of Palestine, one would find nothing comparable which would help pinpoint the time at which the change occurred and explain its circumstances. If the Phoenicians were not the brothers of the Jews, why is it that the language spoken and written by them does not belong to a typically African group, but is virtually pure Hebrew?

On the map, Phoenicia occupies a very small space, about 150 miles long and only a few miles wide. Yet its ships carried the products of the Egyptian and Chaldaean craftsmen, and those of the Phoenicians themselves, to the furthest corners of the ancient world. It thus gave other peoples models to imitate and processes to follow; its example and practices influenced the minds of all the peoples with which Phoenician merchants did business. Scholars differ about the precise nature and the effects of Phoenician influence, but none of them questions the importance of the role played by them

as manufacturers and instruments of communication. For this reason, everything pertaining to this remarkable people deserves attention—the origins, and expansion of the Phoenician cities, their institutions and beliefs—if one wishes to understand the special nature of its role and its civilizing mission.

Left: Carthaginian mask (5th century BC). Below: votive offering from Mount Lebanon (same period).

*Phoenician funeral amphora which had contained
the body of a dead person in the fetal position.*

Facing and below: Phoenician sarcophagi, at Byblos.

Left: lid of a Phoenician sarcophagus (National Museum, Beirut). Right: the Phoenician remains at Byblos.

Left: Phoenician funeral urn (National Museum, Beirut). Below: terra-cotta bas-relief depicting the head of a Medusa (Syracuse Museum).

Phoenician house, as seen by an artist of ancient times.

2　Settlements and dependencies

Egyptian documents first mention the Phoenician cities during the 18th dynasty, about 1600 or 1700 BC. For example, we have the report of an Egyptian officer, under the 12th Theban dynasty, who visited the Dead Sea basin; he mentions no names of Canaanite tribes. On the other hand, a fictitious account of a journey made by an Egyptian official to Syria, towards the end of the reign of Ramses II—contained in a valuable papyrus in the British Museum—describes how he went as far as *Helbon,* the modern Aleppo, returning by the Phoenician coast. He mentions Beirut, Sidon and Avatha, the ruins of which are now known as *Adloun,* finally reaching the "marine city of Tyr" which, to him, seems to be a small town perched on a rock in the middle of the waves. "Water is taken out to it in boats, and it has a great abundance of fish", he says.

It is reasonable to assume that, after their arrival in Syria, the tribes must have spent two or three centuries moving about the country looking for suitable places to settle and building the walls of their cities. This would mean that they first arrived towards the 19th or 20th centuries BC.

According to Herodotus, the Tyrians replied to his enquiries that their town had been inhabited and its temple to Hercules built 2,300 years before. On the basis of such information the first settlement on that site would have occurred about the middle of the 28th century. One should make due allowances for local vanity: having become the most important city in Phoenicia, Tyr was anxious to seem as ancient and venerable as possible, so as to make everyone forget that Sidon was of much more ancient lineage.

All we can say with any certainty is that, when the grat Theban Pharaohs began to campaign in Syria, the Phoenicians already occupied the coast of the country, where they had founded the greater part of the cities one associates with their history. These were, from north to south: Arad or Arvad (Ruad), Marath (Amrit), Simyra, Arka, Gebal, the Byblos of the Greeks (Djebeïl), Beryt (Beirut), Sidon, Sarepta (Sarfend), Tyr, Aco (St. Joan of Arc) and Jope (Jaffa). All of these sites had been so well chosen that all but a few of them are still inhabited today. Indeed, even during the worst of the racial or religious wars or the periods of greatest fanaticism, almost all of them kept their inhabitants.

Of course, with the exception of Beirut, their population in modern times is far from what it used to be in antiquity. Even so, the number of inhabitants never fell so low that Sidon, Tyr, Aco and Jope ceased to be quite important administrative and market towns. More remarkable is the fact that, though numerous conquerors passed through the coastal area down the ages, and people from equally numerous races settled there, not one new urban or trading center has been established there over the past two thousand years. The ancient Canaanite cities, dilapidated though they may be, are still the only cities the country has; moreover, they have kept their ancient names, virtually unchanged, despite the centuries which have elapsed since that time.

The national traditions, which were preserved in the form of cosmogonies by Sanchoniathon, depicted Beirut and Gebal as the two oldest settlements on the coast. Gebal claimed to be the oldest city in the world, having been built at the very beginning of time by the god El. Initially the Gibblites seem to have exercised real authority over the rest of the Phoenicians; however, it was not long before another city, situated further to the south, Sidon, that became the "first-born of Canaan". To begin with it was merely a fishing village, whence it name *Tshidon*, or fishery. "Originally it occupied the northern slopes of a small headland reaching obliquely towards the south-west. The harbor, which was so famous in the ancient world, is formed by a low chain of rocks stretching from the northern end of the peninsula and running parallel to the shore for several hundred yards. The nearby plain is well irrigated and covered with such beautiful gardens that the city had been known as *Sidon the city of flowers*". (Maspero).

Sidon soon had two rivals, Arad in the north and Tyr in the south. Arad stood on an islet some distance from the mainland. Strabo describes it thus: "Arad is a rock about seven stadia in circumference, completely surrounded by the sea. It is entirely covered with dwellings, and is still so densely inhabited that the buildings are several stories high. The people drink rain-water which they store in barrels, or water shipped across from the mainland". There was said to be a fresh-water spring in the

22

strait between the island and the coast; when their water supply ran out, in time of war for example, they used to send divers down to replenish their stocks in this way. The people of Arad had made themselves masters of the whole of the area of the coastline facing them, including Gabala, Paltos, Karne and Simyra. Apparently, their rule once extended as far away as Hamath, on the other side of the mountain, in the valley of the Oronte.

While the Arvadites thus were the undisputed masters in the north, the south of Phoenicia was equally completely under the sway of the Tyrians, who ruled the area between the mouth of the Leontes and the land of the Philistines. For many centuries the other cities in this region were mere dependencies of Tyr. *Tsor* means rock; the later form of the name, *Sour,* was thus closer to the original theme than the Greek version, *Tyr,* which was used by classical authors to the exclusion of all others.

Tyr, like Arad, was chosen for the advantages of its island position; the first Phoenician settlers found that the rocky island was separated from the mainland by about a thousand yards of water, so that a few strokes

of the oar would get them ashore. At the same time, though apparently narrow, the strait was quite sufficient for defensive purposes, protecting Tyr from the designs of any foe who was not the master of the seas. It withstood the oriental conquerors, the kings of Niniveh and Babylon, and Alexander the Great found that he had to build an artificial causeway out from the mainland in order to take it. Thenceforth, Tyr was only a peninsula.

The building of the mole had other effects beside that sought by Alexander; it blocked the natural flow of current-borne sand along the coast, thus causing the harbor at Tyr to silt up rapidly. The only one left today, in much reduced state, is that formerly known as the *Sidonian port:* it can only take a few shallow-draft vessels . . . As for the other harbor, or *Egyptian port,* it has been so thoroughly buried that arch-

eologists who have studied the topography of ancient Tyr on the spot cannot agree on its precise location.

The island, or rather group of islands, which were later joined together with landfill operations to form the surface area of Phoenician Tyr provided the inhabitants with only limited living space. To the south, the sea seems to have reconquered some land which had been formerly gained at its expense by the accumulation of large amounts of fill behind retaining walls; today these walls are partly under water. As was the case at Arad, the houses were tall and huddled together. However, even when one allows for the extreme density of population on the island, it is difficult to suppose that such a small area could ever have contained more than 25,000 people.

There is little reason for surprise

24

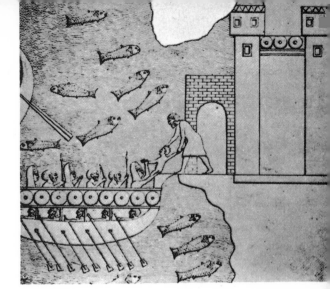

Remains of Tyr. Right: Phoenician ship landing (bas-relief, 6th century BC). Below: reconstruction of Phoenician ship, from ancient bas-relief.

Two streets in the ancient city of Ugarit, in Syria.

in these results, which are based on statistical calculations. Apart from anything else, there was another part of Tyr on the mainland facing the island itself; it bore the same name and was certainly at least as densely populated. It was there that the overland caravans unloaded their merchandise. One should also remember the peasants and slaves living in the scattered farms and villages of the nearby plain, which was admirably cultivated. In time of peace, the city of Tyr itself was doubled or even trebled by the additional inhabitants of the mainland section and the those living in the hinterland, with its agricultural wealth. Mercantile island cities are known to be capable of having an importance which is altogether out of keeping with their actual size. The great historian Ernest Renan quotes the example of St. Malo, in Brittany, a town occupying a situation much like that of our Phoenician city; on a rock measuring less than a third of Tyr, it used to accommodate more than 12,000 people, and was a notable shipping center.

When one thinks of the advantages of the situation of Tyr, close to the mainland but separated from it, one is inclined to believe that this must have been one of the first places settled by the Phoenicians, who had already shown, while in the Persian Gulf, a preference for the security provided by island sites. Tyr may well be as old as Sidon, but Sidon was the first to grow and prosper. Neither the tenth chapter of the Book of Genesis nor Homer mention Tyr.

Phoenicia was not a compact nation occupying a vast territory continuously throughout its entire length: it would be a mistake to compare it to Egypt, Chaldaea or Assyria. It was really no more than a series of ports, to each of which was attached a narrow urban strip. These cities, situated about one or two days' march from each other, were the center of an essentially municipal life, like the Greek cities. When their independence was threatened by the formidable Egyptian, Assyrian, Babylonian and Persian monarchies, or later on by the Greeks, the Phoenician cities, each of which had its own local dynasty and its own constitution, never succeeded in uniting in a confederation which might have been able to withstand outside pressures. The only link between the cities was their original ancestry, their com-

mon language and script, their business relations, community of interests and similarities of customs, beliefs and rituals.

Until the Macedonian conquest, and more particularly the spread of Greek culture, erased all differences between them, it seems that there were three fairly distinct Phoenician worlds.

In the north, there was the area dominated by Arad, which is barely mentioned by the Greek and Roman historians. This part of Phoenicia was certainly very old, because the Arvadites were among the sons of Canaan in the genealogical table of the Book of Genesis. However, we know very little about its fortunes or its life. Their silence is easily explained: this group of cities was shielded and as it were hidden by Lebanon, which separated it from the valley of the Oronte and Lower Syria. It was thus out of the mainstream of Egyptian and Assyrian rivalry over the area. Moreover, it seems that the Arvadites, being content to leave the risks and benefits of far-off adventures to others, confined their navigation and trade to nearby waters, from Cyprus to Rhodes and the length of the northern coasts of Asia Minor. Their

27

business activities had made the inhabitants of this part of Phoenicia very prosperous. The coast to the south of the island curved to form an open bay, which must have looked something like the modern Genovese Riviera: wealthy villages and small towns, the most prominent of which was Marath. The rich shipowners of Arad had their country houses, their farms and their tombs on the mainland. According to Strabo the island measured only seven stadia in circumference, or about 1,400 yards; it was already quite small for the crowds which were compressed into the space behind its tall and powerful fortifications; it could clearly not accommodate the dead.

Gebal, or Byblos, was the center of another Phoenician world which kept its own unmistakable identity

Left: remains of a statue at Byblos. Right: Punic ceramic work, front and side view. (Cagliari Museum, Sardinia).

until the final days of paganism. Here, religious feelings seem to have been more intense and more prominent than in the rest of Phoenicia. As Renan puts it: "Byblos seems to me, on the whole, to be a sort of Lebanese Jerusalem." Their mentality and also their language made the Giblites, of all the Phoenicians, the ones most similar to the Hebrews. In the great inscription of Byblos,

Facing: figure on a pillar in the temple of Byblos. Right: remains of the temple (with Roman columns added). This temple dates from the 3rd millenium BC.

which is one of the most precious monuments of Semitic epigraphy, king Jehawmelek, towards the year 500, addressed his great goddess, Baalat-Gebaïl, in terms which could well have come from the mouth of an Israelite; he presents himself, in the Biblical expression, as a "just king who fears god". Later on, the mysteries of Astarte and Adonis, as well as the orgiastic cult of Tammouz, which were so popular in Syria throughout the Graeco-Roman period, were celebrated precisely in Byblos and the Lebanese valleys under its control.

To the south we have the most representative part of Phoenicia: Sidon and Tyr. It was here that the typically Phoenician genius manifested itself most clearly; it was here that the Phoenicians showed their brilliant grasp of business and industry, of navigation, their wonderful ability to adapt to the most diverse environments and to establish relations with the most barbarous tribes and to generate new needs amongst them. When one talks of Phoenicia, its rapid expansion and the influence it had over the Western peoples, one is really talking of Sidon and, above all, Tyr. The other towns were able to provide sailors to

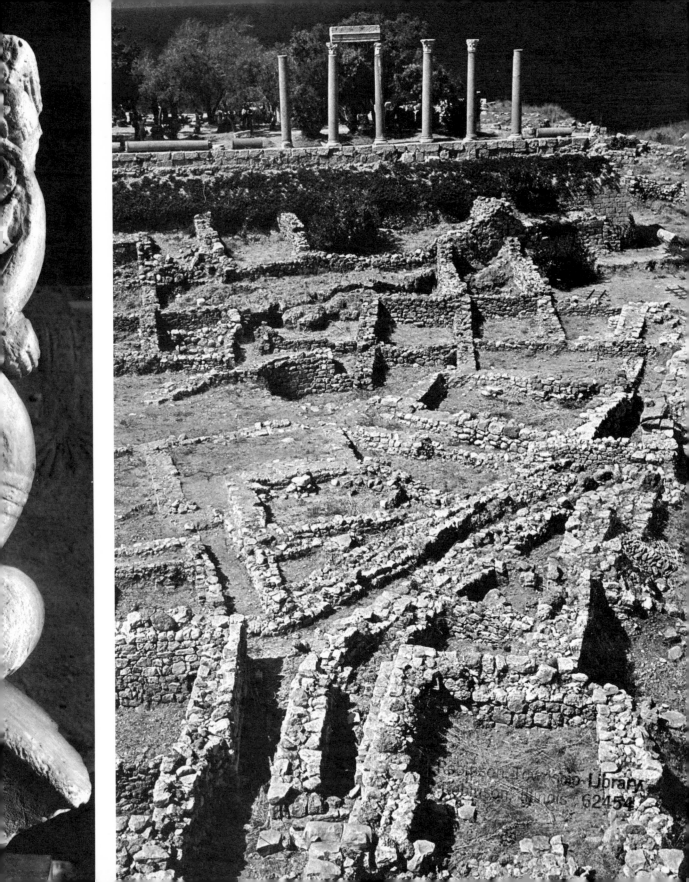

Clay figurines from the 5th century BC, found at Sidon.

Our knowledge of the institutions of the Phoenician cities is very poor; we know virtually nothing of their political and social life. It seems likely, however, that they must have had a régime like that which we find in a number of European cities which, centuries later, had the same ambitions as the Phoenician cities: the Hanseatic towns and the Italian republics such as Venice and Genoa. Wherever the demands of large-scale maritime trade concentrated capital in a small number of hands, and where the profits to be gained from such trade stimulated men's audacity, sustained their energy and enabled the shrewdest, boldest and most active among them to amass huge fortunes, a powerful aristocracy inevitably came into being. The appearances of power were often left in the hands of a popular assembly, or of hereditary or elected princes, though the reality of power, in the form of wealth, was jealously kept in the hands of the aristocracy. The cities differed in that, depending on the time and the circumstances, this aristocracy would either open or close its ranks, moving towards democracy or oligarchy.

Where did Tyr and Sidon fit into this pattern? This is a difficult question to answer. We are a little better informed—or perhaps one should say not quite so ignorant—about the large Tyrian colony in Africa, Carthage. One may safely assume that the daughter kept many of her mother's traits and much of her mood. Accordingly, on the basis of these analogies, the internal régime in the main Phoenician cities must have been strictly oligarchic.

However, as can be seen from the Greek historians and from inscriptions, these cities also had kings. In Arad, for example, there was a dynasty in which the names of Amiel and Jerostratus alternate. In Sidon there was a royal family which was probably as old as the city itself; its reign was interrupted more than once, but, at times of crisis its prestige was invoked as a way of putting an end to internal strife and rivalry.

Tyr seems to have been the most turbulent of all these cities. According to tradition it had several kings, whose names have come down to us; however, like the Jews before Saul and like Carthage, Tyr used to practise the system of *suffetes*, or judges; in many instances, two of these magistrates performed the kingly function at the same time.

Whatever their title, these hereditary princes or fixed term or life consuls could not have had more than a limited authority, which was always in jeopardy. In this respect one should recall the situation of the Doges of Venice and Genoa. The true masters of the cities were the heads of the leading families, or rather of the leading business houses. In Phoenicia as in Carthage or the Italian republics with comparable systems, these persons, who were the custodians of the national wealth and the masters of huge business empires, used to form what really amounted to a senate, regardless of the name it was actually given.

All of them were experienced in business and had the habit of command; each of them had dozens of ships, hundred of sailors, workers and agents working for them. One of these merchants, through the fleets he dispatched each spring and the banks he had set up, might have a monopoly over trade in an area much larger than Phoenicia itself, while another might have gold or tin mines in some remote northern islands or Western territories. In this way the interests of the nation became merged with those of the ship-owners, since they provided it with

The bastions at Byblos (about 2500 BC).

34

steadily increasing markets, and those of the manufacturers who gave it what it needed for highly beneficial trade. There was thus no matter having to do with the future or prosperity of the citizens which could not be dealt with by these rich merchants and navigators who, through first-hand experience, knew the entire Mediterranean coastline and the peoples who lived along it. It was inevitable that such councils attracted to themselves the greater share of whatever power was going. All the most important decisions were taken by the more influential among its members.

However, even when the Phoenician cities appeared, from the historical evidence, to have kings, they were really small republics, aristocratic in nature. It was in Phoenicia that municipal liberty made its first appearance in the ancient world and first demonstrated its strength. It brought into being something which the great urban masses of the oriental world had never known—the citizen, passionately devoted to the independence of his small country and ambitious both for himself and for the society he lived in. By thus exalting the individual's feeling of his own personal worth, this system

Figures from the necropolis at Sidon (now in the National Museum, Beirut).

37

made him capable, when the need arose, of prodigious efforts and dedication. Renan has this to say about Tyr: "It was the first city to defend its autonomy against the formidable monarchies which, from the banks of the Tigris and the Euphrates, came close to destroying the life of the Mediterranean. Even when the whole of the rest of Phoenicia had been subdued, this rock held out alone against the vast Assyrian war machine, withstanding hunger and thirst, until after several years, Salmanasar and Nebuchadnezzar withdrew from the plain.

One cannot fail to be moved as one walks across the isthmus now covering the narrow strip of water which for so long guaranteed the freedom of Tyr. One hundred, and also two hundred years before the Greek victories this was the scene of *Medic Wars* which were almost as glorious as those of the 5th century, and which Tyr sustained all alone."

Through this heroic resistance Tyr has become pre-eminently the city which represents the ambitions of the Phoenician race and its accomplishments. However, it was not the first to open up the sea routes and even when its ships out-

numbered those of the other coastal cities and its captains were unrivalled for their boldness, it was not alone on the seas. Phoenicia never had what we would call a capital city. During the Roman period Tyr and Sidon vied with each other for the title of *metropolis,* or mother of all the other Phoenician cities and founder of Phoenician civilization. While Tyr could claim a more distinguished record of service, Sidon could boast of a much greater antiquity. The first maritime ventures and the first trading posts far from Syrian territory were associated with the period of Sidonian hegemony.

Like the whole of Phoenicia, Sidon had accepted without resistance the suzerainty of the Theban Pharaohs, who were then masters of Syria. The tribute the Phoenicians paid to these overlords was not too high a price for the right to call at all the Delta ports. The relations which they had thus bought with Egypt guaranteed the Phoenicians a dual monopoly which they preserved for many years and whereby almost all the raw materials or manufactured objects which Egypt obtained from Asia passed through their hands and, likewise, a substantial portion of the export output of Egypt's

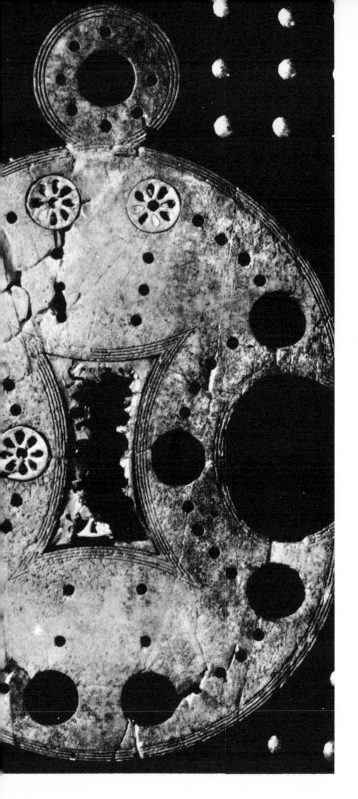

highly fertile and skilled industry was handled by them. As officially appointed suppliers and privileged agents of Egypt, the Phoenicians were in an excellent and exceedingly profitable position. Moreover, as the empire of Ramses was then the leading military power of the Middle East, they benefited greatly from their ability to invoke the powerful protection of the Egyptian princes and generals in Syria and the whole of Asia Minor. Meanwhile, at sea, it was advantageous for them to "fly the Egyptian flag", as it were, and to enjoy both the protection and the prestige of these formidable conquerors.

As for the presence of the Phoenicians in Egypt and the role they played there, a German scholar, Brugsch, has made some interesting observations. He showed that the Syrians were no mere foreign merchants, outside the pale of Egyptian society; papyri dating from the 19th dynasty contain many names of Semitic origin which belonged to officials of the Pharaoh's court. The same scholar has proved that a certain number of gods of Asiatic origin entered the Egyptian pantheon under the same influence about this time. The principal gods and god-

desses concerned were Reshep, Bes, Qadesh and Anta.

With the help of this state of vassalage, which did nothing to hamper their freedom of movement, the Sidonians began to visit the shores of the Eastern Mediterranean. In the north they settled on the southern coast of Asia Minor; they occupied strong positions on the islands of Cyprus and Crete, from which they could easily reach the Sporades and Rhodes, in one direction, and the Cyclades, in the other, while at the same time never losing sight of the mainland and its distant peaks. They seem to have landed quite early at Thera (*Santorin*), at Melos (*Milo*) and at many other points in the archipelago. Maybe it was about this time that they sailed as far north as the group of islands of Thrace, to Thasos, where, for many years, they operated several mines. It has been suggested that they even passed through the Straits, as far as the Black Sea, looking for copper and iron, and, in the Caucasus, for tin.

They were more active in Boeotia than in any other part of the Greek mainland. This is borne out by the myth of Cadmus or the *Oriental* (from *Kedem*, orient) who was thought to have brought the alphabet to Greece and to have founded the city of Thebes. Traces of the Phoenicians can be found in the Argolis, in the Peloponnese. However, their preferred place of settlement was the island of Cythera, adjacent to Laconia, where they had warehouses from which their merchandise could be moved quickly to all the markets of the neighboring peninsula.

Emboldened by their success, the Sidonians soon ventured out into the open sea, entering the second Mediterranean basin, bounded by Greece and the Greek islands, on the one hand, and Italy and Sicily on the other. In Africa they built Utica and Kambe, on the site where Carthage was later to rise. Risking the rough

Left: the remains of the Phoenician city of Ugarit. Facing: sculpted stone (Cagliari Museum).

waters of the Adriatic they reached, at this early date, certain points of southern Italy and Sicily. In all probability they had already taken Malta and Gaulos (*Gozzo*), where they found excellent sheltered harbors in which their ships could take refuge and seek replenishment.

About the year 1000 or 900, supremacy shifted from Sidon to Tyr. After it had been captured and sacked by the Philistines, Sidon took a very long time to recover. Yet this city had already done so much for the glory and the cause of the Phoenician nation that the name *Sidonian* remained, for many years to come, the common name of the entire race, both in Syria and further West. In their official documents, the princes who reigned at Tyr used the title of King of the Sidonians.

The first Tyrian kings mentioned in history were Abibaal, a contemporary of David, and his son Hiram, friend of Solomon. Hebrew, Greek and Roman authors have preserved the names of several other princes, though it is not always easy to determine their precise sequence and dates. One thing is certain: Tyr pursued the work commenced by Sidon, only on a larger scale and with greater daring. In the most fertile

41

part of the north African coastline numerous Tyrian settlements were founded, to become rich and populous cities: Hippo, Hadrumete, Leptis, and, in about the year 800, the "new city", (*Kart-hadast*) which the Greeks called Carchedon and the Italians Carthago.

On account of its remarkable position Carthage grew rapidly, but it never forgot that it was the daughter of Tyr. Every year, a solemn delegation left the colony and went to offer a sacrifice in its name in the most august of the temples in the metropolis, the Melqart temple. After a victorious war, Carthage sent one tenth of the booty to that same temple. If no grand plan for combined action was forged between the two cities, and no joint defense arrangement was worked out, it was simply because such operations were not viewed with favor by the Phoenicians. However, there were always cordial and close relations between the merchants of Tyr and Carthage, no matter where they might be. Their business dealings were closely interwoven, and they habitually reached almost tacit agreements in order to squeeze out foreign competitors such as the Greeks and the Etruscans, keeping the most lucra-

tive deals for themselves. There was no need for written commitments or an exchange of formal promises. This was the kind of agreement that is sealed by bonds of kinship, language and worship, and by an identity of inclination and hereditary habit. Morever, they were joined by the strongest bond of all: they had the same interests, passions and hatreds.

Despite the growing prosperity of Carthage, Tyr remained, for more than two centuries, the most opulent and the most powerful of the Phoenician cities. When its great African colony was just coming into being, Tyr had already begun to take possession of the third Mediterranean basin, stretching from Sicily and Italy westwards. Its vessels travelled regularly along the coasts of this region, calling at its greatly increased number of naval establishments. One can form an idea of the extremely early date at which trade relations were first set up between Tyr and Italy from the words *Serranus, sarranus,* which remained in the Latin language until the classical period. These words are drawn straight from the true Semitic form of the name of Tyr: *Tsor, Tyrius,* which is cognate with *Serranus,*

42

came to be used in Rome only much later, when the Romans had been influenced by the Greeks, who had turned *Tsor* into *Tyros*. Yet the presence and indeed the persistence of the word *Serranus* shows that the Italians, even before they had been in contact with the Greeks and learnt their language, had already had relations with the Phoenicians, in the form of the Tyrian merchant fleet. During its steady movement westwards, Tyrian sea-borne trade had called at the large island of Sardinia, where it found an abundance of various metals. The Tyrians made a harbor for themselves in the magnificent roadsteads of Caralis, now *Cagliari,* while on the west coast they founded trading posts which later became the towns of Nora and Tharros.

From these ports they could sail to Spain calling, at the Balearic Islands or hugging the Mauretanian coastline. For the Phoenicians the attraction of Spain resided above all in its mines, the most readily apparent seams of which had probably been worked by the indigenous population. By following the southern coastline of Spain the Phoenician navigators reached Calpe, or the Straits of Gibraltar, where they found themselves confronted by a boundless new sea and what seemed to them to be the outer limits of the inhabited world. Their collective memory long recalled the fears which they felt, despite their great daring; they were obviously frightened by the enormous size of the waves in the Atlantic and by the rise and fall of the tides. They hesitated

43

on the brink of the unknown. According to a tradition which was current at Gades, it was only after they had drawn back twice that they eventually decided to settle beyond the straits which the Greeks called the Pillars of Hercules. A third expedition, under a bolder captain, then went ahead and founded, on a small island close to the mainland, a colony which later became famous under the name of Gadira or Gades (*Cadiz*). The position of this island, with its houses huddled together in a confined space must have reminded the first settlers of Tyr and Arados. It became a fertile breeding ground for mariners and soon achieved a level of prosperity which Strabo found reason to admire as late as the first century AD.

Security was provided by the island position of this new settlement, while the proximity of the mainland facilitated business. The Phoenician merchants thus soon were doing business with the peoples of Betica, the Turts, or Turdetans described by the Greek and Roman historians. It has been suggested that one of the forms of this ethnic term might be cognate with the word *Tharsis*, which Jewish writers certainly borrowed from Phoenician usage.

There is some reason to believe, however, that this name was first used by the Syrian sailors to denote southern Italy, and that, with the passage of time, Tharsis moved westwards as the Phoenicians found their horizons expanding in that direction. Its meaning was never very precise. When the Tyrians were at the peak of their power, it represented the whole of the territory bordering the Mediterranean in the west: modern geographical nomenclature has a similar phenomenon, as the term *West Indies* has been used for centuries in a rather special way, given its etymology.

In any case, whatever the origins and etymology of this word, there can be no doubt that for the Phoenicians it was quite important. For example, their long-distance vessels were called *Ships of Tharsis*. These vessels were more solidly built, with a higher tonnage than those which worked the Syrian coast and the islands of the Aegean. They were more sea-worthy and their bigger holds could accommodate much more cargo.

Unfortunately it is not this type of craft that we see in the bas-reliefs of the Sargonides, in which there are representations of Phoenician galleys. Some of them, with their rounded hulls, look like freighters for use in coastal waters. The others, with a spur, are clearly warships.

*This curious sculpture deates from the earliest period of the
Phoenician occupation of southern Spain (Seville Museum).*

4 The Persian threat

The Sanish trade soon produced such excellent results that the entire coast east of the Straits became dotted with Phoenician trading posts; the main ones were Malaca (*Malaga*), Abdera (*Almeria*), Carteia (*Algeciras*). There were other less important posts, which have either been referred in writings of the period or whose existence can be surmised, all along the western coast as far as the foothills of the Pyrenees. The valleys of the hinterland and the fertile countryside of the area known today as Andalusia provided the Phoenician merchants with a variety of goods, of which metals were easily the most valuable to them. Ezekiel (Chapter 27, verse 12) had this to say about Tyr: "Tarshish was thy merchant by reason of the multitude of all kind of riches; with silver, iron, tin and lead, they traded in their fairs."

Of all these metals the one the Phoenicians valued most, and the one which brought them the most profits, was tin. The ancient world relied more heavily on bronze than on any other metal, for all domestic and military purposes—and tin was essential to the making of bronze. The fact that they were now masters of one of the sources of tin was of in-estimable benefit to the Phoenicians. Long sea passages did not raise the price of merchandise as much as overland transport covering the same distance. Throughout the Middle East, in Greece, Syria and Egypt, Spanish tin sold more cheaply than tin brought to market by caravan from the Asian hinterland. This difference in cost accounted for its commercial success and enabled those who were the sole owners of this valuable ore to amass huge fortunes.

The expansion of Tyrian commerce into the Western Mediterranean was certainly an inspired move, because, to the east, the seas which had been their exclusive domain for so many years were now gradually being closed to them. Greece was growing, and its population had discovered that it had a penchant for sea-borne trade. During the two or three centuries after Tyr had replaced Sidon as the most prominent Phoenician city, the competition in the Aegean Sea became truly ferocious. Phoenician merchandise was still being bought, but there were now other sources of goods, both ordinary and luxury. The day had gone when they could combine the benefits of piracy and those of trade, and abduct, from tribes incapable of resistance or pursuit, young people or women who they then sold as slaves elsewhere.

The inhabitants of the islands had now built their own ships and resumed ownership of their territory and their ports; the rich silver mines of Siphnos and Cimolos could no longer be operated for the benefit of foreign owners. The island of Thasos was slightly remote from the mainstream of these events, and the Phoenicians had thus been able to hold out there much longer; yet, at the end of the 8th century, they lost it too, having been expelled by a colony of Parians. Milet and its colonies had long denied them access to the straits, and the Ionians, under the Saite princes, began to whittle away at their European clientèle. About this time, the Greeks began to settle in Italy and, shortly afterwards, in Sicily. At the head of a large force of Corinthians and Corcyreans, Archias founded Syracuse in 733, and virtually the entire coastline was divided among other Hellenic settlements. The Phoenicians were in charge only at the western tip of the island, in the three towns known to the Greeks as Motya, Kepher, later called Solunta,

and Machanath, which the Greeks called Panorma.

However, the woes of Phoenicia did not end there, as life was becoming difficult along the Syrian coast. After the disappearance of the last of the Ramessides, a weakened and divided Egypt had withdrawn towards its home territory, leaving Syria without the prestigious Egyptian army for its protection. The decline of Egyptian power was a severe blow to Phoenicia, which now could not withstand the increasingly militant Assyrians. In the 9th century it began to pay a tribute to the kings of Niniveh.

Why did Phoenicia fail to reach an accommodation with Assyrian domination, as it had once done with the Egyptians, and was to do later with the Aechemenids? The fact is that the Assyrian conquerors, with their religious fanaticism, tyrannical harshness and their greed, must have made extreme demands which offended the pride of the Tyrians and ran counter to the interests; the tributes which they were asked to pay were too heavy, and the temples of the gods which had presided over the fortunes of the Tyrian navigators were either threatened or actually desecrated by

48

the worshippers of Assur. Whatever the reason, however, the Tyrians resisted the fierce Assyrian legions on several occasions even though it was left entirely to its own resources and the other Phoenician cities had, as they usually did, surrendered without a fight. For several years running Tyr withstood all the efforts of Salmanasar V and Sargon. Sennacherib compelled it eventually to receive a king appointed by him, and, under the last princes of the dynasty, the city seems to have accepted a subordinate status.

When, after the fall of Niniveh, the Chaldaean Empire had succeeded the Assyrian Empire, Phoenicia quickly sought an alliance with Judaea and, above all, with Egypt, in order to resist the new masters of the area. Egypt was beginning to show signs of recovering its lost greatness, under the Saite princes, and evidently sought to restore its former control of Syria. Unfortunately Apries was defeated, Jerusalem was taken, and Tyr was besieged by the troops of Nabuchadnezzar for thirteen years. Once again, the ancient master of the sea eventually forced the enemy to raise the siege and come to terms (574); however, the sheer length of the blockade had

49

Group of gilded bronze statues, from the Temple of the Obelisks, Byblos.

done considerable damage to Tyrian trade. Caravan-borne merchandise was no longer reaching its stores, its manufacturers were idle, it was running short of sailors and the fight to survive was draining its strength. Sidon, which had resigned itself more readily to vassalage, had taken advantage of circumstances in order to regain its former supremacy. However, it was still a critical period for the whole of Phoenicia: while it was committing itself to coalitions which were being formed in Syria against the Ninivites and the Babylonians, the Greek and Etruscan fleets were supplanting the ships of Phoenicia on many markets.

Accordingly, when Cyrus had become sole master of the whole of Asia Minor, after the fall of Babylon, the Phoenicians, like the Jews, were eager to accept Persian domination. The Aechemenids were not religious fanatics; they allowed the peoples in their empire a great degree of freedom and their financial demands were moderate. The Phoenicians were treated particularly well, as the Persians, having no navy of their own, needed one to fight the Greeks, and were unable to rely on the cordial cooperation of the fleets of the Ionian cities of Asia Minor.

50

Left: Punic-Berber stele (Bardo Museum, Tunis). Right: woman's head on a Phoenician sarcophagus (Louvre, Paris).

Left and right: Punic steles (Bardo Museum, Tunis).

Phoenicia therefore gained a dual advantage by making its ships available to the satraps of the great king: it was able to satisfy its grudge against a hereditary enemy and against the competitors who, over the centuries, had whittled down its sphere of action, while at the same time deflecting into its own ports a part of the royal wealth, as the officers and crews of the Phoenician war fleet were paid out of the imperial coffers. Until the Macedonian conquest, the kings of Persia had no subjects more faithful than the Phoenicians.

On only one known occasion did the cities of the Syrian coast refuse to cooperate with Persia: this was when Cambysos, after the conquest of Egypt, wanted to embark on an expedition against Carthage. According to Herodotus, the Phoenicians declared that it was impossible for them to take part in such a campaign, "because they were linked to the Carthaginians by the strongest of oaths, and that, if they were to fight their own children they felt they would be violating the canons of their blood and their religion". Their reluctance was quite understandable, as Carthage, in the late sixth century, was busily founding,

in the western Mediterranean, a colonial power of which the metropolis could well be proud. It was clearly out of the question for Phoenicia to dampen the dynamism of that branch of the Phoenician race and to hamper the growth of commercial prosperity which was profitable to both Tyr and Sidon because of their business relations with the ports of Africa.

Left: Phoenician tomb, 1st century BC, at Amrit (Syria). Below: cave of the chief of a Phoenician colony in Palestine dating from the 3rd century BC (Beit Djebrin).

57

5 The glory of Carthage

Carthage was lucky to be situated so far from the principal centers of Hellenic civilization. Even when, in the 8th century, the two eastern basins of the Mediterranean, at least in their northern sections, began to be essentially Greek seas, Carthage remained undisturbed in the third basin, in the western seas where the Greek colonies, being remote from their base, had never been very numerous or powerful.

It was to preserve its supremacy in that part of the world until the 3rd century BC, when the Romans inherited the Greek political legacy. However, until the final battles in which it was eventually destroyed, Carthage was able to play a highly important and original role. In the words of one historian, "by virtue of its geographic situation, the city of Dido belonged to Africa and to the West, while its customs, language, civilization and the origins of its inhabitants all place it in Asia and the Middle East. It was the furthest outpost of the Asian world in the western Mediterranean; it was the means whereby eastern civilization, before that of Greece and Rome, reached Africa, Gaul, Spain and even the British Isles."

The region in which the other Sidonian and Tyrian colonies we have mentioned were founded was modern Tunisia, or what the Romans called the *African province*, an area renowned for its fertility. The Phoenician settlers found an established population there of mixed composition, in which it is thought that the race—close to the Egyptians—from which today's Berbers are descended was dominant. The superiority of their industry—perhaps aided by remote bonds of kinship—enabled them to exert a great influence over these tribes, to whom they taught agriculture, which, like all the manual arts, had been taken to high levels of excellence along the shores of Syria. Ernest Renan has found evidence, near Tyr and Sidon, which shows that the Phoenicians had an agricultural technology far superior to that being used by the *fellah* of today in the same region.

North Africa, however, had much vaster plains and far better soil than the narrow coastal strip of Palestine. The wheat produced there soon became a major export item; at the same time the peasants from the hinterland learned the language of the merchants to whom they brought their grains and fruits, in exchange for fabrics, jewels and the

Left: funeral statuette painted ochre and pale blue, height 10 inches (Bardo Museum, Tunis).

tools which were made or sold in the town bazaars. Their relations became constant: a great deal of inter-marriage must have taken place, thus giving rise to that people which, with its strong Semitic elements, was called *Libyphoenician* by the Greeks.

It was with the aid of these persons of mixed blood that the Carthaginians were able to succeed in an enterprise which even their Tyrian forebears had not attempted. In two hundred years, from the end of the 9th to the end of the 7th centuries, they conquered, inch by inch, the entire region between Syrtis Minor and the frontier of Numidia. Besides the coastline, they occupied the hinterland as well, founding numerous towns and settlements which, like the Italian and Roman colonies at a later date, were induced, by the privileges accorded to them, to take the side of the metropolitan power against the natives. Hitherto, the Phoenician settlements had been little more than depots and trading-posts, with only small outlying areas. Carthage, on the other hand, through political deftness, became the master of a rich and spacious territory inhabited by several million people. As for the other Sido-

nian and Tyrian cities of the coast, most of which were older than Carthage, they continued to be known as *allies,* it being understood that Carthage alone presided, in perpetuity, over this confederation and was in charge of its naval and military forces.

The Sidonians and the Tyrians had never had an army. More often than not their trading posts had been set up on rocky islets which were adequately protected by the sea; a few ships served to guard the straits. When it became necessary to go ashore to the mainland to establish depots for foodstuffs and merchandise, a strong wall protected the post from sudden attack. In addition, so as not to find themselves repelling assaults too frequently, they used to pay the barbarian chieftains of the coastal areas an annual amount: this was the procedure used, centuries later, by the European merchants who sought to trade freely on the territory of a petty local king on the Guinea coast, for example. They discharged their obligations by handing over barrels of rum, glass beads, gunpowder and old rifles. The Phoenicians were not averse to providing the natives with items which they happened to find

highly desirable: wine, for example, was as eagerly sought after by these tribes as alcohol was later on. Using a cool, calculating approach to the matter, the Tyrians preferred to buy the use of several hectares of land in this way, instead of having to conquer and defend them violently.

Circumstances compelled Carthage to take quite a different course, however. Having decided to occupy the country, it then needed an army. The first members of such a force were provided by the very tribes which were to be subdued. The high rates of pay which the Carthaginians could offer attracted men of all the races which lived in its territory or neighboring regions; they recruited Libyphoenicians, Numidians and Moors, while the citizens of Carthage itself acted as officers. To begin with, Africa provided all the men needed for this army. Later on, however, during the great struggle against the Greeks of Sicily and the Romans, it became necessary to have recourse to all those who were prepared to fight in return for money: consequently, virtually all the peoples of the Mediterranean coast were represented in the great companies of mercenaries which, under the command of Hamilcar,

Hasdrubal and Hannibal, challenged Rome for supremacy in the ancient world.

Even before such huge forces had been raised, Carthage, early in the 6th century, already had something which no Phoenician city had ever had: a territory and an army. It was thus able to cope during the ten-year duel between Tyr and Chaldaea, which had prevented the Phoenician city from supplying and defending its overseas posts. Danger signs were visible everywhere: in Betica, the Turdetans suddenly revolted and attacked the Phoenician posts, massacring the African settlers established by Tyr in the valley of the Betis. Things were made much worse by the distinct suspicion that Greece was in some way responsible for these events. As early as 640, Coleos of Samos had thrust boldly into these remote shores and had been lucky enough to escape. On his return home, Coleos had praised the wonders of Betica and the treasures of Gades. Thenceforth, there was not a single Ionian captain who did not dream of the day when he might land at *Tartessos,* the Greek form for the name Tharsis.

While trying to find his way to Spain, a Phocaean Greek named Euxenos had landed in southern Gaul near the mouth of the Rhone, where he founded Massilia, site of the modern Marseille. In 578, the Rhodians and the Cnidians, following the same route, landed in north-eastern Spain and founded Rhoda (modern *Rosas*); however, it was the Phocaeans who drove westwards with greatest zeal. What Herodotus tells us about the very cordial reception accorded the Phocaeans by the king of Tartessos, whom he names Arganthonios probably coincided with the siege of Tyr and its reluctant abdication. Obviously the Greeks drove a less harsh bargain and must have been nicer than the Phoenicians. In any case, about this time, fortune indeed seemed to smile on their youth and their ambitions. In Sicily they began to threaten the last three towns kept by the Phoenicians.

From one end of the Mediterranean to the other, all the Phoenician sailors, merchants and settlers began to look anxiously and imploringly towards Carthage. If Carthage did not take over the affairs of Tyr, Phoenician commerce, which had now been expelled from Sicily, and was under severe restraints in Spain, looked like coming to an untimely

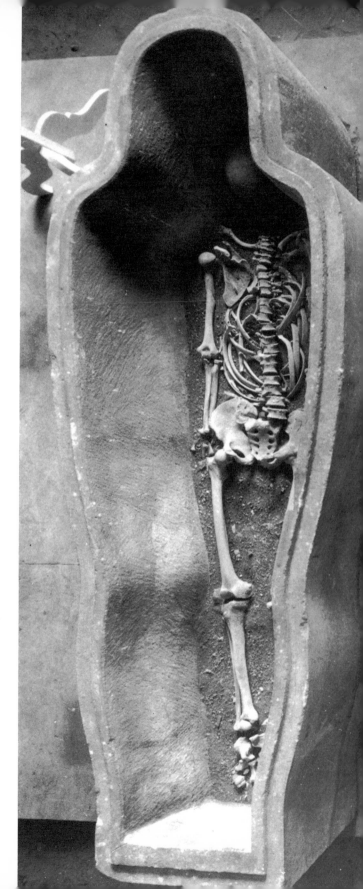

Facing: Phoenician sarcophagus, and, upper right, reproduction of its upper section.

end. Carthage met their appeal, and handsomely, realizing that times had changed. In the days when the Sidonians and Tyrians found the shores of the Mediterranean sparsely inhabited by barbarous tribes, the security of their trading posts had been an easy matter. Now, however, the world was becoming more populous, the native tribes had learnt the use of iron and bronze weapons, and, lastly, throughout the European coastal areas of the Mediterranean the Greek civilization was making itself felt rapidly. It had already outstripped the Phoenicians in all the spheres of art and ideas: a new situation therefore required new modes of action.

Carthage did not hesitate. Instead of taking a merely defensive approach, which would have cost it a good deal of ground annually, it struck out in a campaign of conquest. The days of monopoly had gone for ever; yet, by its policies, it won for itself a privileged position in western waters for three centuries to come, keeping control over the most productive land and the bulk of trade in the Mediterranean.

A great expedition was sent to Spain, where it removed the threat to the coastal cities and took the val-

64

ley of the Betis, as well as the mining areas which were of capital importance. A large number of Libyphoenicians were moved into the area and established there as settlers in order to keep the natives in check. In the event, they inter-married with them. A system of government and colonisation which had been used in Zeugitania and Byzacena was applied to Betica. In order to ensure their strategic and commercial communications with Spain, both by land and by sea, the Carthaginians took care to fortify substantially the cities called by the Greeks the *Metagonites,* which formed an unbroken chain along the coast of Mauretania as far as the Pillars of Hercules. They had been previously founded by the Tyrians in order to provide ports of call for their ships on the Gades route. Moreover, Carthage formed a close relationship with the Numidians, hoping thereby to ensure their respect for these posts, which served as a source of recruitment of mercenaries among the

Below: entrance to a Phoenician tomb in the Cadiz area.

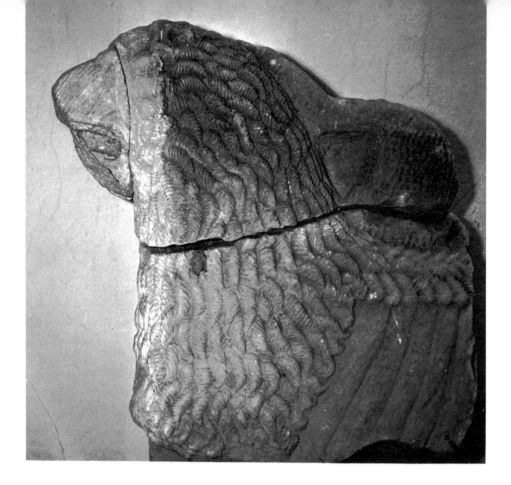

warlike tribes of the interior.

Encouraged by these first successes, the Carthaginians soon decided to dispatch to Sicily an army which enjoyed the connivance of the natives from the hinterland, the Sicules and the Sicanes, who were increasingly alarmed at the expansionist tendencies of the Hellenic colonies. Within a short while, the Carthaginians made themselves masters of the western part of the island and of the central highlands, driving the Greeks into the north and east. The cities which still belonged to the Phoenicians, now no longer threatened, as a result of this brilliant offensive, were given sound defenses, complete with garrisons. Wherever the Tyrians had hitherto put only warehouse-guards, the Carthaginians now installed troops.

An equally great—and equally successful—effort was made to recover the former Phoenician supremacy in the waters between Sardinia and Spain, where Phocaea and its colony Massilia posed a serious threat. It was the Phocaeans who, in

66

Left: sculpture of a lion (Guadalquivir region). Facing: Carthaginian statuette.

order to offset the advantage the Phoenicians had gained by their control of a part of Sardinia, had founded, in 556, the town of Alalia or Aleria at a superb site on the east coast of Cyrne (Corsica). From here they could control the entire Tyrrhenian Sea and Gulf of Liguria.

The capture and destruction of Phocaea by Harpagos, in 547, during the Persian conquest of Ionia, far from weakening the Phocaean settlements in the West, actually increased their importance. Once a colony, Massilia now became a metropolis. In the words of Thucydides: "Fugitives from the ruins of Phocaea—energetic individuals, fearless sailors, fled to Massilia or Aleria with such of their possessions as they could save. For the local Greek population this was a great boost, the effects of which were not long in making themselves felt. The Phocaeans and Massaliotes occupied and destroyed the trading posts which the Phoenicians had founded on the Ligurian coast, the west coast of Spain, in the Ebro region and near the Pyrenees. Their warships even defeated those of Carthage on several occasions; they won a distinct superiority in these waters, and kept it for some time."

Punic stele, with two arches, dedicated to a human couple; width 2 ft. (Bardo Museum, tunis).

Might not the Greeks take the bulk of the highly fruitful Spanish trade? Was there not some danger that, once they had become masters of Corsica, they might find the allure of the Sardinian mines irresistible? Carthage could not allow such ambitions to develop freely, as the issue was almost one of life or death. It was therefore decided that a new effort would be undertaken in order to regain the kind of control which Carthage had already won for itself in Sicily and Betica. This time, fortunately, allies were available to help.

This was the time at which the Etruscan civilization reached its apex. This strange people, which left us so many monuments and inscriptions, but so few clues as to its origins and language, lived for the most part in Tuscany, though there were also Etruscan cities in the Campagna. These two groups of the same people, separated by Latium, where the power of Rome was growing, had to retain their mastery of the sea if they were to be able to communicate freely. The Phocaean stronghold on the Corsican coast opposite Tuscany was, to them, a threat, and even an affront. Both Etruscans and Carthaginians had the same apprehensions and same enemies, and an agreement was soon reached between them.

The Etruscan fleet sailed from Populonia, the main port of Tuscany; it joined the Phoenician fleet and, in 536, the combined naval force moved on Aleria. What the Ionians lacked in order to play the role they had hoped would be theirs was numbers; they confronted the attacking force and won the battle. However, finding themselves exhausted by their victory, with no time to make good their losses, they had to evacuate Aleria. The former inhabitants of the town fled either to southern Italy, where they founded Velia, or to Massilia.

Corsica lacked the fertile plains and, in particular, the mineral wealth of Sardinia. The Carthaginians were content to keep a few naval outposts there, and they abandoned the island to the Etruscans. However, they flattened almost all the cities which the Ionians had started to build along the Spanish coast. They returned to Liguria, where the rock of Monaco was one of their fortresses. Massilia survived with some difficulty, until the naval victory scored by Hieron, tyrant of Syracuse, in 474, over the Etruscans

69

at Cumes. This brilliant victory enabled the Greek navy to recover its freedom of movement in the Tyrrhenian Sea, the Gulf of Lion and the Ligurian Sea. The Massalians never seem to have attempted to accomplish the grand designs which they had worked out a century before. They confined themselves to building up an economy in southern Gaul, leaving the islands and Spain to the Phoenicians of Africa.

By the very nature of things, a kind of tacit or formal convention came into being among these trading nations: each of them stood to gain from trade arrangements which increased the number of deals taking place. Massilia even had a Carthaginian trading post; such, at least, is the evidence gained from the scale of sacrificial charges in the temple of Baal, drafted in the Punic language, which has been found at Marseille (the former Massilia). It was clearly engraved on the territory of Marseille, because the stone on which the inscription occurs is from a quarry at Cassis, a nearby town.

No longer bothered by their former fears about the doings of the Phocaeans and their armed competition, the Carthaginians set about completing their system of strategic

Jug placed inside a sarcophagus, and probably intended for use in sacrificial ceremonies. (Bardo Museum, Tunis). Following pages: two Carthaginian steles.

70

positions in the western Mediterranean. After some setbacks they took Sardinia, where they did much to promote the development of agriculture, as they had previously done in Africa. The island reached a level of prosperity which it was never to have again. When the Romans conquered it, Sardinia, which had long been sparsely populated, wild and unhealthy, had been converted by three centuries of Carthaginian rule into a rich, well cultivated and flourishing island, with a large population and numerous towns.

The leader who had completed the subjugation of the Sards, Magon, also occupied the whole of the Balearic Islands. On the island of Minorca he founded a town which became one of the main naval outposts of the republic; its name, *Port-Mahon*, remains virtually unchanged to this day.

By the end of the sixth century BC, therefore, Carthage had come to occupy a dominant position in one half of the Mediterranean; indeed, this sea was already proving to be too small for its merchants and its sailors, who ventured with increasing frequency beyond the Pillars of Hercules, into the great Atlantic. The Tyrians had, of course, been

Votive offerings from ancient Carthage.

Phoenician oarsmen, and picture of a merchant ship, on a stele.

there before them, but had been less intrepid. Acting on orders from the Senate of Carthage, a navigator named Hannon explored the coast of Africa as far as the 8th degree of northern latitude. The official account of Hannon's journey, which was preserved in the temple of Baal-Hammon at Carthage, has been preserved for us intact in a Greek version.

After this expedition the entire coast of Africa from the Straits to Cape Noun was colonised, and, according to various accounts, some three hundred trading posts were set up, among them Tingis (*Tangiers*) and Sala (*Rabat*). Whereas most of these were eventually abandoned, there were some, such as Cerne (the island of *Arguin*) which remained lively commercial centers, with large annual fairs. During this voyage of exploration the Carthaginians discovered the Canary Islands and landed at Madeira. A passage from the writings of Scylax even suggests that they tried to push on further west, reaching the Sargasso Sea, but, finding the surface covered with vast quantities of seaweed, they thought better of it and turned for home.

Had it not been for the wars with the Sicilian Greeks and with Rome,

which later put a great strain on Carthage, a Phoenician Christopher Columbus might well have discovered the New World twenty centuries ahead of time. After all, Tyrian sailors, long before Vasco da Gama, had rounded the Cape of Good Hope and circumnavigated Africa in the year 600, at the expense of King Nechao of Egypt.

While Hannon was heading for the south Atlantic, another captain, Himilcon, was reconnoitring the western coasts of Gaul and Spain; he also landed in Britain. One wonders whether the Tyrians had ever gone that far: claims to that effect have never actually been proved. However, it has been established that, during the Carthaginian period, ships from Gades went to an archipelago called the *Cassiterides*, or "isles of tin"; these were the Scilly Isles. In return, they took the natives salt, vases and bronze weapons, as well as pottery. It seems likely that they must also have landed at various points on the coast of Cornwall and Ireland, but, true to their custom, they preferred to settle on these small islands where they felt their security was better assured. On the islands they set up markets where the inhabitants of the neighboring

76

landmasses could bring their merchandise and do business with these foreign traders.

This Atlantic trade was a monopoly which the Carthaginians were careful to protect. Their pilots jealously guarded the secrets of the winds, currents and anchorages, while at the same time spreading rumors about the extreme dangers involved in navigation along these routes so as to discourage the opposition. Those who were not so easily deterred, and who actually dared to follow in the wake of the Carthaginian vessels were taking a great risk, since their masters did not hesitate to kill, if necessary, in order to keep curious eyes at a safe distance. When such an encounter occurred, if they felt stronger than the intruding vessel, they would turn and chase it, boarding it and slaughtering all on board. If boarding were out of the question they would readily risk their own lives rather than give away their vital secrets. Strabo tells of a Phoenician ship off the west coast of Spain which, seeing that it was being followed by a Roman vessel, deliberately went aground on underwater rocks, causing the Italian galley to do likewise. The navigator in question managed to swim ashore; when

Three grotesque masks,
found in Sardinia.

he returned home he was awarded the price of the boat and the cargo he had thus sacrificed, as compensation.

Such methods were not applicable in Italian waters, where the Carthaginians had to be content with being admitted to ports which were equally accessible to Etruscans and Greeks. The Carthaginians had decided, at an early date, to refrain from settling on the mainland of the peninsula, choosing instead to oc-cupy positions which dominated the approaches to it, such as the island of Lipara, from which they could monitor movements in the Strait of Messina and the entire coastline of southern Italy. From these forward positions they would sail either on missions of piracy or to do business, as circumstances demanded. Business was definitely the more profitable of the two activities, as the Carthaginians were almost the sole source of supply for certain articles

Reproduction of seats and furniture, in terra-cotta, from Carthage.

from Africa or the Middle East.

Conventions were drawn up in order to facilitate and support these relations. Aristotle was aware of the treaties concluded between the Etruscans and the Carthaginians, and Polybus has preserved for us the translation of the first of the agreements signed between Carthage and Rome, on behalf, respectively, of the metropolis and of the allies of Rome. It dates from the year 509, one year after the expulsion of the Tarquins. Excavations in Etruria and Latium have confirmed this historical evidence; the burial grounds of these countries have provided archeologists with a number of objects which bear, as it were, the stamp of the merchants of Carthage.

It was about this time that the greatness and wealth of Carthage reached their apogee, its affairs being conducted with the greatest possible prudence and, at the same time, decisiveness. We shall not discuss here the major wars with Sicily in which Carthage was involved early in the following century, about the same time as the Medic Wars were taking place in the eastern Mediterranean. We shall, with all the more reason, refrain from giving

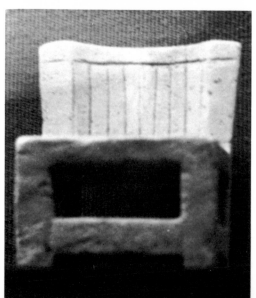

an account of its long duel with Rome, at the end of which it was finally devastated, despite the genius of generals such as Hamilcar or Hannibal. Long before the final fiery collapse—witnessed by Scipio and Polybus, who were reminded thereby of the noble and melancholy verses of Homer—Greece had already begun to show its ascendancy. From the middle of the 5th century, its art had reached perfection; henceforth the Hellenic world could be said to derive no more than raw materials from the eastern trade, whereas the superior forms it had created had gradually been imposed on all the peoples of the Mediterranean area.

Carthage had undergone these slow but powerful influences quite as much as Syria, which was much closer to the main centers of Hellenic civilization. From the mid-4th century Tyr was ruled by Strato, whose passion for the arts of Greece had led to his being nicknamed the *Philhellene*. The same had happened to Carthage, which, while engaged in a murderous struggle with the Greeks of Sicily, yet found time to cart off the statues decorating the Sicilian temples and install them in its own temples and public squares. It also

copied Greek coins, from the end of the 5th century onward—or perhaps one should more accurately say that it had them struck specially by Greek artists; moreover, long before the Roman legionnaires forced their way in through the breached defenses, Greek architects had wormed their way into Carthage. The temples which collapsed during the final blaze, the temples of Baal-Hammon and Tanit, cannot have kept much of their ancient Phoenician character, having been reconstructed many years before, in the style made fashionable by the great architects of the period of Alexander and his successors. One reliable source of evidence in support of this conclusion is the Ionic style of the porticoes in the naval harbor. No remnants of these buildings have survived to this day, but traces of Greek influence can be discerned even in the ornaments on the steles dedicated to Tanit, "*face of Baal*", so many of which have been recovered.

In this curious collection, alongside divine types and symbols which can be explained solely in terms of the Phoenician religion, one finds fragments and themes of a wholly Greek sculpture, crudely reproduced as one might expect in the case of

such monuments of popular devotion. The miniature temples before which the worshipper stood, or which contained the emblems of the divinity, had a triangular façade, on fluted pillars with scroll-like capitals. The pediment was adorned with acroteria.

These acroteria are also to be found on another pediment, the center of which is occupied by a mother-goddess. While the tympanum is unusually high, the cornice, on the other hand, is decorated with a very characteristic row of ova. An unmistakably Ionic column supports a bust of Tanit, resting on a crescent, in one of the more curious of these small monuments. In the original, of which we now possess only fragments, a cornice with ova and spearheads was placed above the goddess's head. This is not pure Greek art, in either proportion or design; but were it not for the presence of symbols such as the crescent,

Colored terra-cotta ewer (Carthage).

it would contain nothing at all reminiscent of Egypt or Assyria, and nothing which could remotely be called Phoenician.

While following the history of Carthage westwards and bringing it up to the time when it merged with that of Greece and Rome, we seem to have lost sight somewhat of Tyr and Sidon. We should not forget, however, that neither the Persian nor even the Macedonian conquest stifled the genius and the prosperity of that hardworking race. Indeed, the suzerainty of Persia had been accepted as a delivrance, in return for which the Phoenician cities always made their fleets available for the suppression of the revolts which occurred periodically in Ionia, Cyprus and Egypt, though it is true that they managed to benefit handsomely from such operations.

However, their loyalty began to weaken towards the middle of the 4th century, when the Aechemenid Empire seemed on the point of collapse. In 316, under Ochus, Sidon revolted and massacred its Persian garrison; through the treachery of its king, Tennes, it was captured, burnt to the ground and emptied of its inhabitants, who were sold into slavery. After the battle of Issus (333), Byblos, Arad and the other cities of the coast hastened to make their peace with their conqueror. Tyr alone heeded its pride more than its interest; it was prepared to accept the suzerainty of Macedonia, just as it had previously been the vassal of Persia, but it refused to allow Alexander, at the head of his guard, to enter the gates of the city, through which no victorious enemy had ever passed. Its resistance was costly: after a seven-month siege it was taken and sacked. The breakwater built by the attackers in order to link it to the mainland changed its position for ever. Mastery of the seas no longer guaranteed its impregnability.

Tyr thereafter renounced the kind of grand ambitions which had long been abandoned by the other cities along the Syrian coast. The Phoenicans were content to be merchants, more knowledgeable, quicker to spot a good deal, more shifty and thrifty, and, therefore, richer than their enemies. As subjects first of the Ptolemys, then of the Seleucids, and later as part of the Roman Empire, they had trading posts in Antioch, Alexandria, Corinth and Athens; later they had one at Pouzzoles, in Italy. In all of these cities they lived in a separate district.

6 Primitiv gods

Little is known about the Phoenician religion. It is true that inscriptions—mainly dedications or fragments of rituals—have revealed the existence of several unknown gods. Some valuable information has also been drawn from a careful study of Phoenician names, most of which consist of composite words containing the name of a divinity. Lastly we have some fragments of the works of Phoenician writers and a fairly large amount of diffuse data occurring in the writings of the Greeks and Romans. Although modern scholarship has done much with this scant material, many points still remain obscure.

The epigraphic texts are terse and dry; they explain nothing. An analysis of proper names produces nothing more than a simple name of a divinity, while the fragments of the Sanchoniathon bear the mark of crude syncretism, and should, for that reason, be used cautiously. The same reserve should be shown towards the material to be found in classical literature, since its authors did not know Phoenicia until it was already in decline, when it was more or less Hellenized; moreover, they may not have fully understood what they saw and heard. Another cause

for caution is the ease with which the classical authors slip into facile assimilations which often prove to be inaccurate.

Phoenician religion had kept many of the attitudes characteristic of primitive societies; more than one of its formulas and rituals had a distinct air of fetichism. The mountains had their gods, or, more precisely, they were worshipped as gods, on account of their imposing mass, the majesty of their gloomy forests, the thunder of their cascading streams, the height of their snowy peaks and the depth of their narrow, somber ravines. This mountain worship should be seen as an expression of the blend of admiration and fear which they instilled in the tribes which, after long migrations, came to settle on the lower slopes of Lebanon, where they saw the vast shadow of the mountains reach out, morning and evening, over the sea and the plain. This form of worship certainly dates back to the earliest days of Phoenician occupation; it is clear, moreover, that it survived for a long time, as can be seen from certain epithets, some of which occur in the Semitic texts, whereas others have been embodied in Greek transcriptions, *Baal-Lebanon, Baal-*

Bronze figurine, probably of a priest (British Museum).

85

Hermon, Zeus Casios. Baal-Lebanon is mentioned in the oldest of the Phoenician inscriptions in our possession—a dedication engraved on a bronze cup, the fragments of which are now in the National Library in Paris.

In the same spirit, sacrifices and prayers were offered to the rocks, caves, springs and rivers: the cave which opens at the end of the *circus* at Afka, and from which the Nahr Ibrahim flows, was one of the most sacred places in Syria for thousands of years. The temple of Astarte, or the Aphrodite of Aphaca as it later became, was demolished by Constantine, but succeeded in rising again after him; there can be no doubt that the worship conducted within it dates back all the way to the beginnings of the Phoenician occupation. Religious sentiment could hardly have failed to occur at such a spot, one of the strangest and most beautiful landscapes in the whole world. Certain trees were also the subject of worship: the Zeus Demarous mentioned by Philon of Byblos must surely have been a Hellenized form of *Baal-Thamar,* the "lord palm-tree."

Here also we must seek the origin of the worship of the *betyl,* which is found throughout the part of the world influenced by Phoenicia. The word itself comes to us from the Greeks, who in turn had taken it, virtually without alteration, from the Semitic *Beth-El,* or "house of god". This was a sacred term which was used generically to denote all sacred stones, that is, all stones which were felt to be impregnated with and animated by a special power, or which were regarded by the populace as the residence of a god. Nothing was more variable than the form of these stones and the degree of religious respect which surrounded them. They were usually conical or ovoid, sometimes pyramid-shaped. In certain sanctuaries they were steles with flat sides. It was claimed, in addition, that some of these stones were aeroliths, a fact which enhanced their reputation.

The spread of the ideas and arts of Greece did not cause the worship of *betyls* to fall into decline. Under the Roman emperors it became more popular and more widespread than ever throughout the eastern provinces. Astarte, who was known in those days as Aphrodite, was represented as a cone in the famous temple of Paphos in the time of Tac-

itus, while at Byblos she was the major deity of the area. On the back of a coin from Byblos struck under Macrin one can see the sacred stone standing in the middle of a courtyard surrounded by porticoes. Another stone worthy of note was the celebrated black stone of Emesus, from the same period; Heliogabalus was its priest before he became emperor.

Betyls were therefore revered, and sacrifices were offered to them, not only on the coast, but throughout the whole of Syria, right up until the last days of paganism. This form of worship surely dates back to the very birth of religious sentiment, and its first manifestations, though the homage paid to these crude symbols was never so intense as during the decadent period of the ancient world. In fact, their very strangeness, with its capacity to arouse curiosity, had a strong appeal for the jaded imagination of the decadent. It was particularly at this time that a crude stone could be regarded as the highest incarnation of the divinity.

What happened was a regression, on the part of society, towards the tastes of childhood, not unlike the corresponding phenomenon in individuals. At the time of the earliest monuments of Phoenician writing and plastic art, the Phoenicians had progressed from the adoration of mountains, trees and erect stones. Towards the end of the Sidonian period, when the ships of Tyr and Sidon were plying the waters of the Mediterranean from one end to the other, the beliefs and the forms of worship of Phoenicia were already different from those of Egypt. There were no sacred animals, and the worship of the dead did not seem to have been such a prominent concern of the living in Phoenicia as it had been in Egypt. The dominant trait was the worship of stars and the great forces of nature, each of which was viewed as the manifestation of the energies and the will of a powerful and mysterious being, a god who was every day responsible for a wide range of phenomena.

This kind of polytheism seems even more abstract and more advanced than that of Chaldaea, and more remote from the phase known today as *polydemonism*. In it, the divine personages are less numerous and have a more concrete existence. It is quite possible that, at this early stage, the notion of a supreme god might have been in the process of

formation—a god situated above the concept of multiple and distinct gods, as it were hidden behind them, and choosing to express through them the ineffable and endless fertility of his life.

Some scholars detect this supreme god in the *Baal-Samaim,* or "Baal of the heavens", to whom the great inscription at *Oum-al-Aouamid* is dedicated. It does occur elsewhere, but in such cases, for example an inscription on the island of Sardinia, it is accompanied by geographical epithet which weakens its general and superior nature. Next door to Phoenicia, the Jews were moving closer and closer to the notion of monotheism, until eventually, as a result of the preaching of the prophets, it reached its logical fulfilment, about the time of the Assyrian triumphs. The Phoenicians and the Jews, particularly those of the kingdom of Israel, lived side by side, and enjoyed close relations; in fact, they spoke virtually the same language, to the point where a man from Byblos would have had little difficulty in understanding the eloquent speeches and the impassioned invective of Elias, Elisee and Isaiah. Yet, there is no sign that the powerful oratory of these prophets and

poets was heard in the coastal cities, or that Phoenicia became associated in any way with the great religious movement which was under way. While it is true that certain expressions of the Phoenician texts seem to suggest that in both Tyr and Thebes thinking had begun to evolve, very gradually, towards the notion of a first cause, the Phoenician people, having no penchant for metaphysics, must have regarded it as no more than a vague and fleeting aspiration.

Their indifference must be attributed in large part to the example and influence of Hellenic polytheism. A number of gods and goddesses landed with the Phoenicians on the shores of Europe, and it was through these navigators that a kind of outline of several favorite ancient divinities was transmitted to the inhabitants of the Mediterranean basin. The Greek imagination further refined the features of these gods and made them seem more alive by giving them a better defined form. Once the Greek genius for the plastic arts had begun to reach the plenitude of its development, the Phoenicians found, with increasing frequency, that several of the gods their fathers had worshipped, and which they worshipped themselves, were now well distributed around the coasts of Greece and Italy. The only difference was that they had been transfigured by the power of an incredible art, and placed in temples of compelling beauty.

Being mariners and merchants, they naturally spent most of their time away from home; more of their life was lived at sea and in remote trading posts than on the narrow strip of coast where they had their base port and their legal residence. During their travels, what most struck them was the elaborate pomp and the high degree of development of an unashamedly pantheistic religion. In all the sanctuaries they saw a reflection of the image of their own principal national deities, only in an embellished and enlarged form. Wherever they went—and they were constantly on the move—they came across the same spectacle. These impressions were not such as would make them abandon beliefs which had so thoroughly captivated the minds of the richest and most civilized peoples of the day.

In this way it is possible to account for a paradoxical phenomenon: the Phoenicians' unawareness of the great religious revolution

Goddess of Fertility.

which was beginning in nearby Judaea, from which they were not separated by either moral or natural obstacles. As shrewd businessmen they kept in constant touch with all inventions and new developments; as soon as any new product appeared on any market they immediately hastened to procure supplies of it for their customers, both near and far. It must have seemed to them a poor policy to espouse the worship of the jealous god of the Jewish prophets—a god who would have nothing to do with any other, who would not share his powers, and who even refused to allow any representation of him in sculptural form. Had he not already, through his hatred of idols and fear of them, prohibited any representation of man and animal? "Thou shalt have no other gods before me. Thou shalt not make unto thee a graven image, or any likeness of any thing that is in heaven above, or that is in the earth beneath, or that is in the water under the earth: thou shalt not bow down thyself to them, nor serve them: for I the Lord thy God am a jealous God, visiting the iniquity of the fathers upon the children unto the third or fourth generation of them them that hate me;" (Exodus, XX).

Another Punic stele; here, a distinct Roman influence is perceptible. (Bardo Museum, Tunis).

93

Such harsh conditions never applied to Greece, which was so enamoured of beautiful shapes; the Christian societies, when they adopted a religion which derived from Judaism, were inclined towards similar feelings, and readily pursued the habits they had acquired while trying to get around this prohibition. Unlike the Greeks, the Phoenicians were not artists, tormented by a passion for the reproduction of beautiful things; yet their own self-interest was what turned them away from doctrines which made such extreme demands. In fact, images were a leading item in their commerce for several centuries. All of the objects which they marketed so abundantly throughout the Middle East, whether of glass or ivory, earthenware or metal, bore images: animals, both real and imaginary, men and gods. The Phoenicians used to manufacture gods for export; on all the islands of the Aegean Sea, and along the coast of the mainland one finds statuettes of the great god Astarte, of Bes, a god which they had probably borrowed from Egypt, and of the dwarf gods which became the Greek pygmies.

Another factor which made it less likely that the Phoenicians would espouse the lofty doctrines being proclaimed in neighboring Palestine was the fragmented condition of the Phoenician race in Syria. Cities which have a strong municipal sense of identity are reluctant to become assimilated in a powerful State; instead, they resist what seems to them to be a decline, with the result that an intense love of a small nation prevented the formation of larger units. This same pattern of thinking had the same effects in the religious domain; peoples whose attitudes were of this sort would have separate gods for each town, which either excluded all others or put severe limitations on their worship. Truly exceptional circumstances were required in order for one of these local gods to be able to break out of his narrow mold and gradually become a national god, or even, with the passage of time, what might be called a "human god". By this latter term we mean a god of a sufficiently elevated character, capable of revealing to the mind of man the infinite wisdom and power which he adores under so many different names.

This is what happened in Greece, where the notion of the city and the

state merged; however, at an early
stage, Greek thought and perception
gave rise to gods who, by virtue of
their generality and the moral values
they expressed, far transcended the
role of special protectors of a given
city or tribe. These gods include:
Zeus, father of men and the gods,
Apollo and Pallas Athenea. This
was because Greece, despite its political divisions, proved able to give
itself a spiritual unity which was unknown in Phoenicia. Greece had
great poets, Hesiod and, above all,
Homer, whom all its sons could re-
cite by heart; it had festivals such as
those of Delphi and Olympia, during which, at least for a few days, all
the Hellenes felt themselves to be
brothers, and united in a common
joy with each other; its art, which
sought to be universally understood,
imparted to its principal types a set
of features which were essentially
the same for each inhabitant of
Olympus. Phoenicia never had this
kind of unity, since these forces
never worked to attenuate the effects
of the sort of dispersal to which it
was doomed by geography and by
the special mode of life it chose to
follow. To a far greater extent than
those of Greece, therefore, the gods
of Phoenicia remained municipal in

96

nature, attached to one fixed point in space, the gods of such and such an expressly named town or sanctuary. Such precise geographical identification of gods could not fail to slow down the development of religious thinking, and was not likely to arouse and inspire the artistic imagination.

Among certain peoples, such as the Greeks, a plurality of gods was due above all to the variety of divine attributes conceived by the mind; in Hellenic polytheism one already has, in a poetic and naive form, a profound analysis of the qualities of being and the laws of life—the brand of theology one would expect to find in a people which later went on to create philosophy. The secondary gods of the Phoenicians, on the other hand, were not the result of such a methodical and felicitous effort of the intelligence, and correspond much more to geographical and political divisions. The divine name most commonly found either in the Phoenician texts themselves and the composition of certain names or in respect of Phoenicia in the historical books of the Old Testament, is *Baal*, meaning "master". This term seems to have been an honorific title applicable to all the

97

divinities; from it derives the word *Baalim*, the "Baals" which occurs in the Bible. There were as many Baals, or *masters*, as there were cities, or places devoted to a particular form of worship. In this system, the Baal adored at Tyr, Sidon, Tarsis and on Mount Lebanon and on Mount Phegor becomes *Baal-Tsour, Baal-Sidon, Baal-Tars, Baal-Lebanon* and *Baal-Phegor*.

Even so, the blurred notion of primordial unity subsisted behind these local denominations, as can be seen from expression such as *Astoret-Sem-Baal,* "Astarte name of Baal", in Phoenicia, and, in Carthage, *Tanit-Pene-Baal,* "Tanit face of Baal". In these and other formulas the term Baal is used, in the form almost of an abbreviation, as the proper name of the supreme god, though it never lost its vaguer and more general sense, which was completed by the addition of the name of a city or a mountain. In this way, Melqart, the great god of Tyr, who was worshipped far and wide as the result of the spread of the Tyrian colonies, was merely the Baal of the metropolis. A dedication found on Malta speaks of "the lord Melqart, *Baal of Tyr*".

The name Melqart, which has

come to us via Greece, also contains another of the honorific epithets whereby the Phoenicians used to designate their main divinity: *Molok* or *Melek*, the "king". Though a frequent component of men's names, it has never been found in isolation, as the name of a god; however, we can form an idea of its value from the role it plays in the formation of the title borne by the tutelary deity of Tyr, the *Melqart* whom the Greeks turned into Meli-kertes, a sea god. Melqart is a contracted form of *Melek-Qart*, the "king of the city", its complete name being *Baal-Melqart* or *Melqart-Baal-Tsor*, "Melqart master of Tyr". The word *Adôn*, or "lord", was used in the same way. It was only relatively recently that it became the proper name of a god, worshipped more particularly in Gebal; this god eventually spread to Greece and became one of the more prominent in the ancient world.

It can be seen from the foregoing that the titles given to the most august of the Phoenician gods were strongly influenced by the geographical element in them, and that, therefore, they could hardly be expected to evoke such clear ideas as were suggested to the Greeks by such words as Zeus, Hades, Poseidon, Hermes and Apollo. Accordingly, they lent themselves much less readily to a plastic tradition. Despite all the hard work done by scholars, it is still difficult to define the concept underlying vague terms such as Baal, Melek, Adon and others like them. An examination of certain epithets and rituals has led some authors to see these gods as gods of nature, worshipped in its most spectacular manifestation, the sun. All the Baalim had this feature, particularly the Baal of Gebal, the Tammouz who was invoked by cries of *Adoni, Adoni* ("my lord"). This famous person, who later came to be viewed by the Greeks as a simple Syrian hunter, was the sun-god himself to the Phoenicians, the star which seems to die each year with the cold season, in order to be reborn in the spring. These festivals in fact contained alternating scenes of mourning and rejoicing, in an order

established by tradition.

Just like Egypt and Chaldaea, Phoenicia also applied the notion of sexual reproduction which they saw in the natural world to the world of their gods, so that goddesses existed side by side with the gods, in couples. Each Baal had a Baalat, or "mistress". At Byblos (*Gebal*) this goddess was worshipped under the name of *Baalat-Gebal,* or "mistress of Gebal". She enjoyed a great reputation along the entire coast, being the source of the goddess Betus whom they mentioned as a Syrian goddess. In Carthage, Tanit was paired with Baal-Hammon, while at Sidon and Tyr Astoret performed the same function in respect of Baal-Sidon and Baal-Melqart.

Of all the Phoenician Baalats, Astoret, or Astarte, as she is called in the Graeco-Roman transcriptions, seems to have acquired the greatest consistency and personal identity. She had already been in existence a very long time before settling on the Syrian coast with the Phoenicians, and accompanying them on their travels to all the islands and shores of the Mediterranean. She is the Istar of Mesopotamia—the same name, slightly modified, and the same attributes.

100

As a counterpart of the male god, Astarte was the goddess of the moon—a pale reflection of the sun; at the same time she was the goddess of the planet Venus, and it must have been in this capacity that she was alluded to by the Jewish prophets when they spoke of the worship of the "Queen of the skies" (*Meleket-has-samaïm*) which must have corresponded to the *Baal-samaïm* or "King of the skies", being venerated as his immortal spouse.

Like nature itself, whose energies were all personified and expressed in her name, Astarte, the true sovereign of the world, in her tireless activity, was constantly destroying and creating, creating and destroying. Through war and scourges of all sorts she eliminated the old and the useless, those who had performed their role in life, while at the same time presiding over the perpetual renewal of life by means of love and regeneration. To strive, under her aegis, to keep alive the flame of eternal desire whereby the species was continued was a meritorious act and a tribute to her; this led to the creation of the rite of sacred prostitution and the custom of attaching to the temples of Astarte those groups of women who, under another name,

continued in Greece—for example at Corinth—the tradition of the Phoenician sanctuaries. Cyprus, Cythera and Eryx, in Sicily, had received from the Sidonians the religion of the Syro-Phoenician nature-goddess. In Sicily, in the first century BC, the temple of Venus at Eryx still had vast land-holdings and troops of slaves of both sexes who, having served the goddess, became freed under her aegis and remained under her protection; they formed a class which had special rights, and those rights were respected by the Roman governors; in Latin they were known as *venerii*. There was a Phoenician inscription from Eryx which was probably an account of an offering to this divinity; however, the stone itself has been lost, and the only existing copy is so bad that the text cannot be reconstructed from it. Having become Greek under the name of Aphrodite, Astarte kept the surnames of Cytherea, Erycina and Cypris in the writings of the Latin poets, almost like certificates of origin. The dove, the most prolific of all birds, was the preferred sacrificial animal in her cult; later on, Aphrodite was pleased to receive this same offering. Terra cotta figurines have been found in Phoenicia, Cyprus and Sardinia representing either the goddess herself or one of her priestesses; with one hand they are holding a dove and pressing it to their breast, as the emblem of the cult of Astarte.

Following the pattern whereby the celestial world is modelled on the natural world, the divine couples then had a son, who is often represented as his mother's lover. Like Egypt and Chaldaea, Phoenicia also had its triads, but these groups do not seem to have been formed with such firmness and constancy as in the two nations previously mentioned. At Sidon, it seems that a bond of this sort united the three prime deities, Baal-Sidon, Astarte and Esmoun, a god later assimilated by the Greeks to Asculapios. Virtually everywhere, at least among the eastern Phoenicians, the feminine element in these divine families was represented by Astarte. Her name was generally prefixed by the term *Rabbat,* or "Great Lady", which was also applied to other goddesses. Anat or Anahit, the Anaïtis of the Greeks, was certainly part of the same conception. The goddess was also worshipped under this name in Syria, whence her cult

passed into Egypt; it is contained in a Phoenician inscription on the island of Cyprus. The name changed, according to the place, but the idea and the feeling behind it remained the same.

Below these great gods, Phoenicia had others, most of which are only poorly understood to this day. *Reshep, Resef* or *Resef-Mikal* was the Phoenician Apollo; at least there is a Cypriot inscription in two languages which identifies it, in its Greek section, with Amyclean Apollo. He had penetrated into Egypt, and, judging by the way he is shown in Egyptian monuments, one would be inclined to see him as a god of war, an Ares or a Mars. Ordinary men's names lie at the origin of the gods *Semes* (the Sun), *Sakon* and *Poumai*, the pygmy god of the Greeks. It is doubtless among these gods and others like them that one should look for the seven *Cabirae*, or the "Powerful Ones"; the worship of these gods was imported by the Sidonians into the islands of Thrace, where it survived until the last days of paganism. As their name suggests, the Cabirae were the planetary gods. They were headed by Esmoun, the "eighth", if one accepts the Semitic etymology of his name.

102

Esmoun was the third person of the triad which occurs, in different forms, in all the cities of Phoenicia. Esmoun was the supreme manifestation of the divinity, the one which embodied all the other manifestations of creative energy, just as the world embraces the seven planetary heavens.

This whole group of divinities was characterised by one distinctive feature: they were all dwarf or child gods, which, from the iconographic point of view, are close enough to be mistaken one for the other. Herodotus had remarked on the strange appearance of these disproportionate limbs, and the short legs supporting an enormous head; he found it reminiscent of one of the forms which Egypt had given to its god Phtah, or, as he was known to to the Greeks, Hephaistos.

It is not surprising that the Phoenicians, being away from home so much of the time, borrowed heavily from foreign religions. Of course, we are not now talking of the original basis of their beliefs: it contains certain conceptions, types and names which they seem to have brought with them from their distant homeland, from the shores of the Persian Gulf where they used to live, and

from Mesopotamia, which they crossed. There are similarities between Bel and Baal, Istar and Astoret which are exceedingly obvious.

Like the other tribes which have inhabited Syria, the Phoenicians had brought to the region all the components of a religion which originally came into being in Chaldaea; moreover, during their nomadic existence over the centuries, they constantly borrowed gods and forms of worship from the peoples among which their merchants worked and which, sooner or later, came to be dominant in Syria itself. There is a substantial amount of evidence of the influence exerted by the great Assyrian and Chaldaean empires at the time when Phoenicia paid tribute to Niniveh and then to Babylon. There is an inscription in Athens in which a Phoenician is entitled "priest of Nergal". A bilingual inscription found at Larnax-Lapithou, in Cyprus, contains a dedication to the goddess Anat, whose name is rendered in Greek as Athenea. But it was above all neighboring Egypt, with which Syria had such close and prolonged relations, which influenced the Phoenician pantheon the most profoundly.

Osiris, Horus, Bast, Harpocrat were worshipped in the coastal cities, not as foreign divinities revered merely by a few individuals. This can be shown by the place occupied in proper names by the names of some of these gods, and by the parallels between them and the purely Phoenician gods; on the model of *Melek-Baal*, one could say *Melek-Osir*. Osiris certainly figured in the Phoenician pantheon, but in a borrowed capacity, as he must have entered it at a fairly recent date, through the natural effect of the close and sustained relations which Egypt had with Phoenicia under the Theban Pharaohs and the Sais, at the time of the Aechemenids and even under the Ptolemys.

Carthage came into being too late, and had preserved too strong a bond with its metropolis for its religion to be markedly different from that of the eastern Phoenicians, from which it differed in only minor ways. The couple of the two principal *Baalim* which were thought to be specially concerned with the protection of the city, consisted of *Baal-Hammon* and *Tanit*, while the addition of Esmoun completed the triad. Baal-Hammon, or "Baal the burning" was, as his name suggests, a fire or sun god. Baal-Hammon was rep-

104

resented as being in the flower of manhood, with ram's horns, with the ram leaning against the throne on which the god was seated. As for Tanit, she was the Astarte of Carthage, a goddess of nature, only under another name, and with a slightly more pronounced sidereal and lunar character. The Greeks identified her with Artemis and the Romans with Juno. Classical authors sometimes referred to her as the "celestial Virgin" or the "genius of Carthage"; Melqart, whom the Greeks assimilated to their Hercules, as a wandering god, the conqueror of Barbary, also had his temple near the harbor, as was the case in all the Phoenician colonies.

Besides these major divinities, the Carthaginians adored others which were less famous, and of which we only know the names: Sakon, Aris, Tsaphôn, and, among the goddesses, Astoret, Illat, and others who are mentioned in the texts only indirectly, through periphrases such as the "great mother" and the "mistress of the sanctuary". During the two centuries preceding the fall of Carthage, that city's religion became strongly imbued with Hellenic elements; however, the features which survived till the very end were certain rites, the cruel nature of which is evidence of the harshness of the Phoenician genius. For them, as for all the other peoples of the ancient world, the sacrifice was the religious act *par excellence,* the act which brought man into contact with the gods and compelled them to repay their worshippers.

It is easy to understand why, among the most primitive peoples, it was felt that the best way to honor a god was human sacrifice; but, as the beginnings of civilization began to remove the harshness from men's lives, the notion of substitution began to gain ground. There were several ways of offering to the gods, and having them accept, an equivalent sacrifice. Sometimes the intended victim was replaced by a domestic animal, a ram, an ox, a bird or a stag, while it was possible to replace this living being by a stone, which became a sort of representation of an imaginary sacrifice which was erected in honor of the divinity.

In Egypt and Chaldaea we have already found traces of human sacrifices; in Greece this was a custom which disappeared early on. Among the Phoenicians, particularly those of Africa, these holocausts persisted as long as the gods in whose honor they had been instituted continued to exist in the popular mind; such sacrifices were still being celebrated among them at a time when they filled the rest of the civilized world with horror. The fact is that the Phoenicians were attached to this practice as a result of a long tradition. The victims of the sacrifice were usually the first-born or the newborn. This was a way of consecrating to the gods the very finest of one's wealth. At one point this custom penetrated into Hebrew usage, from Phoenicia; the Bible speaks of children who were passed through the fire in honor of Moloch, in other words, the fiery and solar principle which the Phoenicians worshipped under different names. According to Tertulian these sacrifices were still being held openly in Roman Africa in the first century AD. In order to stop them, or at least to make them clandestine, the emperors, starting with Tiberius, had to decree the death penalty for any priest who took part in such ritual murders.

The enthusiasm with which these holocausts were held must have had something to do with the thought that fire purifies all it touches, and removes all stains. The Carthaginians were driven by complex sentiments to renew these sacrifices with redoubled vigor whenever they found themselves in critical circumstances. Their fanaticism became exalted, and, from the open hands of the gigantic statue of Baal-Hammon the children of the most noble families, delivered by their own parents as expiatory victims, fell into the flames below, which reached up to the legs of the colossal monument.

The originality of the Phoenician religion lies above all in the violent and impassioned nature of their rituals, and in the contrasts which they contain. Scenes of orgiastic delight such as frequently occurred in the lobbies of the temples of Astarte were followed, within a short time, by extremes of funereal passion characteristic of barbarous devotions and by the murderous sacrifices which they produced—not to mention what we later find in Greece, since here men's souls are less gentle and their feelings less temperate than they were in Egypt! One should remember that the Phoenicians were above all businessmen and navigators; there was no place in their life for literary culture and philosophy, nor for the pleasures of art. They tended to relax rather abruptly from the tension of profit-seeking and

danger on the high seas by promptly engaging in a crazed round of pleasures barely had they set foot on the shore. Then, restored and rested, they would set about their business again with renewed relish. If, at any time, things looked like going bad for them, if their vessels were threatened by storms or the Punic armies were defeated in battle, they were only too ready to do horrendous things in order to regain the favor of their gods. This people of merchants, who were so very hard on their debtors, envisioned their gods as implacable, demanding creditors; this accounts for the terror which caused them to sacrifice so many young lives in the prime of their infancy.

Acting under the influence of sentiments attributable to national custom, the Tyrians and Carthaginians thus imparted to their forms of worship a very special character; however, the gods they adored were not of their own creation, and, consequently, when they wished to give them a shape they proved incapable of inventing anything new. These gods, most of which had been imported from Mesopotamia, were then clad in the Egyptian style. Phoenicia became a civilized entity during the centuries when it was considered as subordinate to the empire of the Theban Pharaohs, and it took from its masters the images and attributes of their divinities. On the Jehawmelek stele, the *Great Lady of Gebal* looks exactly like an Isia-Hathor; here we also have a bronze, also from Syria, which does not seem to have been made in Egypt, but in Syria. It must be an image of Astarte, her head crowned by the disk of the planet and the horns of the moon, yet the uraeus stands up on the goddess's forehead as if she were an Isis. Moreover, it was the type of the child Phtah that Phoenicia had taken over in order to give a body to its Kabirae and its Pygmies.

Ancient tablet with cuneiform characters, from Ugarit (Damascus National Museum).

Left and below: Carthaginian inscriptions. The stele reproduced on the right bears the above inscription on its pedestal. It was found in Malta, and represents the offering of two brothers to the god Melkart.

Ancient sarcophagus found at byblos. It bears the first known inscription in the Phoenician alphabet.

7   The invention of the alphabet

Cuneiform script, in the more ancient monuments in which it has been found, allows us to imagine quite clearly the time when it was merely a depiction of objects, a pure exercise in draftsmanship. As for hieroglyphics, they have never lost this attribute. Certain special traits of the Egyptian sculptors' work can even be explained, to some extent, by the habits acquired by the scribe's hand as he formed the plain images, in such large numbers, on papyrus, wood or stone. Nothing similar happened in Phoenicia. There is no trace of a period in which the Phoenicians used ideograms to express their thoughts; it was by inventing the alphabet that they learned to write.

It is no longer thought that they invented it all on their own; but much thought has been given to whether they took the signs to which they attached phonetic values from cuneiform or from Egyptian script. Most scholars are inclined to take the view that they borrowed from Egypt, about the time when the Hycsos of Manethon, a population similar to the Phoenicians, was dominant in the Nile Valley, or at least in the Delta. One thing is certain: the whole of antiquity paid tribute to the Phoenicians for the progress they had made. The opinion of the ancient world is nicely expressed in these two lines from Lucan:

Phoenices primi, famae si creditur, ausi

Mansuram rudibus vocem signare figuris.

Such literary evidence is fully borne out by the findings of science. We know of no alphabet properly so called before the Phoenicians; all alphabets which have been preserved in monuments, or which remain in use to this day, come more or less directly from the first alphabet which was put together by the sons of Canaan, and then spread by them throughout the known world.

Whether the Phoenician letters were borrowed from the cursive script then used in the papyri of the first Theban empire, or whether they came directly, for the most part, from some of the signs of monumental script, the fact is that the invention of the alphabet goes back much further than had been previously supposed. The very ancient alphabetic inscription of Mesa, king of Moab (896 BC) indicates a well-established tradition of writing. The shape of some of the characters even

113

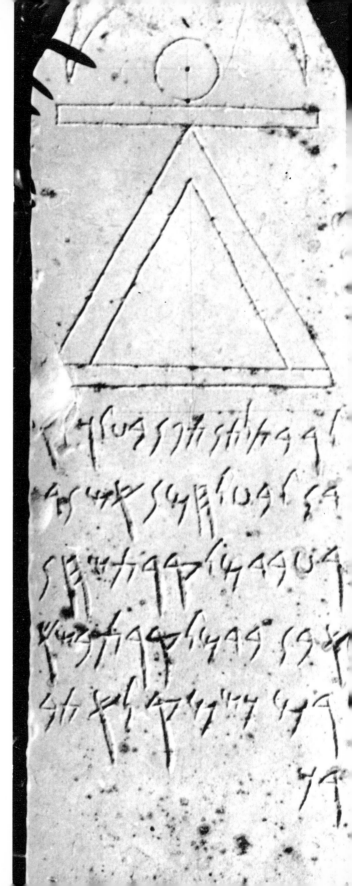

suggests a script which had been in use for a very long time, and which had become a little "worn". There can be no question of proposing even approximate dates for these phenomena, though it does seem likely that the Phoenicians already had an alphabet when they started sailing in the eastern Mediterranean. In any case, this secret was known to the Sidonian sailors who first landed on the shores of Greece and the islands.

Thenceforth, on all the shores visited by Syrian vessels, the savage forebears of the Greeks, standing in a circle around these strange merchants, would watch with fascination, once the deal was concluded, as they made up their accounts; leaning forward eagerly so as to get a better look, they would point out the scroll which the merchants would take out of their robes; then they would watch the *kelem,* soaked in ink, which ran over a clay tablet or a papyrus. Such an unsophisticated audience could not possibly have understood the sense of these myriad lines, repeated in an endless succession of combinations; they must have thought, for quite a long time, that some magic operation was in progress, and must have duly

114

worried at the thought. How many centuries were required for them to grasp the purpose and the nature of these mysterious figures? We cannot say; but, as soon as the light shone in their minds, they immediately wanted to try to use these signs to represent the sounds of their own language.

How had the Phoenicians themselves been induced to undertake the work which led to the creation of their alphabet? Since they readily borrowed the arts and industry of Egypt, why did they not also borrow its script? The most probable answer is that they found it too inconvenient, too complex and too difficult to learn. After all this was a script which contained some ideograms which were meant to be understood literally while others had a figurative meaning; some of its phonetic signs represented syllables or individual letters; in certain circumstances the same word might appear as a single ideogram, while in others it might have to be broken down into its parts, thus requiring the use of several characters. The same idea could therefore be expressed by a range of means open to one's choice; such an arbitrary system was highly confusing for the reader and could give rise to all manner of misunderstandings. The people which had invented this system and practised it for thousands of years was not even aware of its shortcomings; there is no instrument which man cannot eventually master, given a long hereditary usage. The scribes in the Ptolemaic and Roman temples sometimes used these characters as if they were deliberately seeking not to be understood, so that the sacred texts should be more obscure. It has been suggested that they might really not have wanted to be understood at all, but this theory does not seem valid. It is more likely that they were trying to show off their dexterity, in the same way as a pianist might sometimes play passages more for their pianistic difficulty than for anything else.

Literate Egyptians, being well trained in this delicate skill since childhood, could honestly admire and praise such ability as a god-sent gift—sent, precisely, by Toth, the god with the head of an ibis. Foreigners attempting to master the arcane script were far worse off. Their task was made no easier by their lack of a native predisposition and the effects of a professional education which began in Egypt at an age when

115

a young mind can make great demands on its memory. It is highly doubtful that anyone from another race ever found his way into the ranks of the Egyptian scribes, or even caught a glimpse of the way they thought.

Even so, the Syrians who had begun to travel to the ports and main cities of Lower Egypt were greatly intrigued by the sight of the Pharaoh's officials and the princes of the nomes, with their writing equipment, noting down the amounts of dues paid at the frontier, and the quantities of grain or the number of head of cattle or poultry being sold at market. This is what they found so admirable—more so than the great monumental inscriptions on the walls of the temples or the sides of the pylones, giving the names of the peoples conquered by the Theban monarchs. Of course, their ambitions were aimed much lower: in a world where others sought to win glory on the battlefield, they merely wished to make money. What mattered to them was that they should be able to master the cursive script. What an advantage it would be for them to be able to use it in order to record, day by day, or even hour by hour, all the transactions begun or concluded, and all commitments entered into! How pleasant it would be not to have to rely exclusively on one's memory, or, worse still, on the memories of one's debtors!

The trouble was that this tachygraphy confronted foreigners with no fewer difficulties than the monumental script; it too used characters of widely differing values, and, in order to use it fluently, one had to be familiar with the hieroglyphs, which the signs expressed in abbreviated form. If this instrument was to be used immediately, the main thing was to reduce its complexity and reduce its script to a small number of characters; but there was only one way this could be done. In any script based on ideograms, the number of signs is certainly not equal to the number of objects perceived or thought about; but it must be fairly close, and any system of this type necessarily pre-supposes a vast number of different signs. The different vowels, in combination with the consonants, produces even more combinations; writing based on the notion of the syllable will also require a large number of characters: the cuneiform syllabary contains about a hundred. The situation is quite different if the sign represents

116

no more than one of the elementary articulations of the human voice, a vowel or a consonant; in all the alphabets we know, there are only about twenty letters which correspond to sounds in which the ear perceives any difference of substance.

The phonetic elements used in Egyptian script included signs of this type, but they had to be set apart from the syllable and idea and object signs. These letters—and no others—had to be taken, and the other, more complicated signs left to the scribes of Memphis. How was such an operation undertaken? Was it clearly intended, from the beginning, that only a number of the Egyptian signs were to be borrowed? Was there a long period of trial and error, or was the alphabet, based on the principle which accounted for its prodigious success, devised by the genius of a single man? We will never know, though this is one problem which is uniquely challenging to our modern curiosity.

In the history of mankind the invention of the printing-press is an important date; but the date of the invention of the alphabet, if we only knew it, would be even more impor-

tant. The task of breaking down words into their basic components and analyzing their nature must certainly have required an effort of intelligence far superior to the idea of forging mobile characters and putting them under a press.

One of the principal merits of the Phoenician alphabet is what we might call its universality. The fundamental articulations of the voice are few in number in any language. It is true that there are some sounds which speakers in certain cultures cannot pronounce at all; one might say that each national keyboard is missing a few notes. However, the one thing which most distinguishes one language from another cannot be expressed in writing: it is the tone or the color of the sounds, the force with which they are emitted and their duration. As for the articulations which scholars classify as local pronunciations, it is very easy, once the method has been found, to note them down with the help of the signs adopted by the Phoenicians, or others based on the same principle.

Each of the national groups to whom the sight of the Phoenician alphabet suggested the use of alphabetic script could doubtless have invented the alphabet on their own,

117

from scratch, with signs created specially for their own language. Yet this is not the way mankind has chosen to proceed in the age-old undertaking which amounts to what we know as civilization. Except when some abrupt blow has snapped the chain, man has always drawn heavily on the discoveries of others, using them, in turn, as a point of departure, rather than wasting his time beginning all over again. He has always felt it was better to revise and improve.

This is exactly what happened to the alphabet: all the peoples who, on land or sea, were in touch with the Phoenicians, borrowed from them their alphabet, and, changing it as appropriate, they adapted it to the requirements of their own languages. The Phoenicians had obtained from Egyptian cursive script both the shapes and values of their signs. Gradually these signs passed to the Hebrews and to the northern Semites, or Arameans, while at the same time spreading through northern Arabia to the Libyans and even the Hindus; in a westerly direction they became adopted by the Greeks and the Italiots, and even the remote Spanish tribes learnt how to use them. Having traversed such huge

distances, it is only natural that these signs changed a great deal, as a result of numerous influences: the habits of the hand, which varied from fast and nimble to slow and heavy, the differences of local conditions and also those of social situations. However, when one refers back to the earliest forms of the Phoenician alphabet and those derived from it, the resemblance and the basic identity of these forms become evident. Compare, for example, the characters of the oldest Greek inscriptions of Thera and those on the Mesa stele, or the bronze goblet which bears the name of Hiram. Such an analysis shows that the outline of the letters is not the only thing which has changed, as some of the values—a minority, it is true—have also changed.

The Phoenician alphabet had no vowels; only the consonants were written, and the reader then had to supply the missing vowels, on the basis of the context. Such a vague arrangement could hardly satisfy the Greeks, whose language relies heavily on vowels in the processes of derivation, as well as in conjugation and declension. The Greeks got their vowels from the Phoenician semi-vowels, and then, finding that these

118

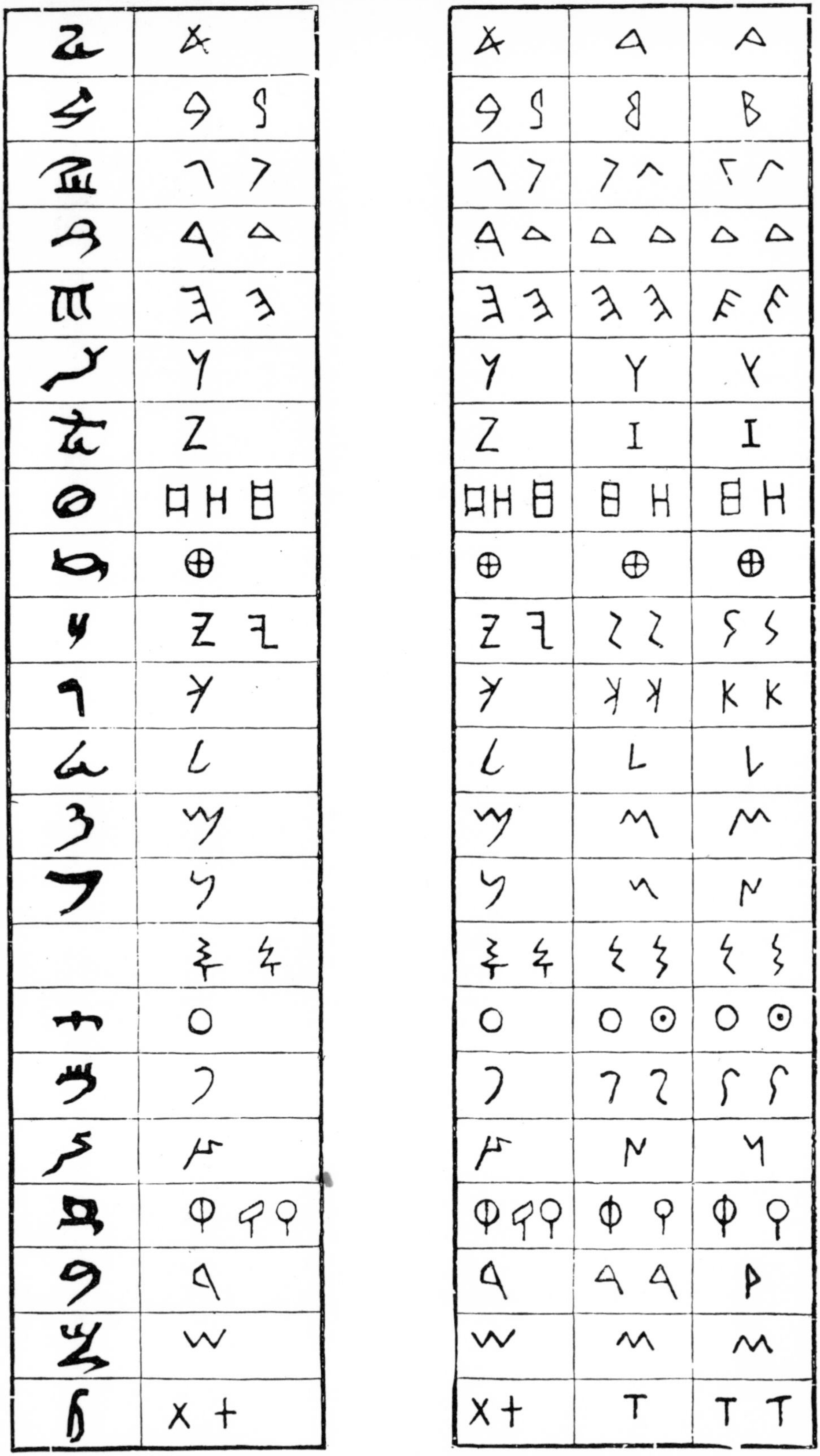

were not enough, they also used the group of gutturals, of which there were many in the Phoenician alphabet, but which would hardly be needed in their own clear and sonorous language: *ioa* and *vav* became *I* and *Y*, *aleph A*, *hé E*, *heth H* and *aïn O*. In the case of *vav*, the Greeks seem to have hesitated somewhat, making several attempts to place it in their own script, as if they had some difficulty in exhausting the content of this letter, which in Hebrew has a vague, floating quality. *Vav* gave rise successively to *digamma* and *upsilon* in Greek, and in Latin to four letters, *F* (corresponding to *digamma*), *U, V* and *Y*.

These observations make it possible to assess the progress made by the phonetic script through the skill of the Greeks; right from the start, the Greeks provided the solution to a problem which had always bothered the Semites, who, despite prolonged efforts over the centuries their languages had existed, never succeeded in recording the vowels properly; at least, they never found a way of doing it using the resources of their original alphabet. The *vowel-dots* of the Jewish rabbis of the 6th century AD were applied in

120

A tomb, Carthage.

a highly artifial way to a language which was essentially dead; it has now been proved that these signs give a very false idea of the pronunciation of the words at the time the Old Testament was written.

Having invented a marvellous instrument, the Phoenicians then proceeded to do little or nothing with it. True, they used it for accounting purposes; but they never expressed in it any particularly immortal thoughts, and had no literature, in the full sense of the word. Their writing seems to have been concentrated on precious stones, which bear only the briefest texts, and on bronze, which has been lost. Ernest Renan has this to say: "Before the discovery of the Mesa inscription one could validly have doubted that epigraphy was in use anywhere among the peoples of Canaan. Steles such as the one at Mesa must have been rare; while the habit of putting inscriptions on monuments, tombs and coins probably came after the period in which they imitated the Greeks."

Renan also points out: "Phoenician numismatics follows the same law: there is no Phoenician coin pre-dating those of Persia and Greece. The inscription of Ech-mounazar is certainly not older, and in any case the clumsy self-conscious style is far removed from the simple and firm manner of the peoples which were accustomed to writing on stone. Instead of the grand style in which the Romans and the Greeks addressed posterity, the only inscription of any note which has so far been found in Phoenicia is merely a rambling tedious account of the fears felt by a small-minded man towards the vat which contains his bones. No feeling for history, and no lofty concern for posterity, only a narrow selfish attitude. Even the manner in which the inscription is carved is evidence of the uncertain nature of the technique used. The artist made two attempts, each time with a different method. Apart from anything else, the monotony of Carthaginian epigraphy is really remarkable. The two thousand five hundred inscriptions found in Carthage are almost all identical, with only three or four exceptions. It seems, in fact, that the inventors of the art of writing did precious little writing themselves. One can safely say, at any rate, that the public monuments of the Phoenicians were without epigraphs of any sort until the time of the Greeks."

Form responds to substance. Besides the words themselves, which are rarely noble or striking, the appearance of the letters is also singularly monotonous and not such as would make anyone take the ideas expressed in them very seriously. Phoenicia had no monumental script: its epigraphic alphabet always kept the features of a cursive script. Not a single Phoenician inscription uses any of the devices whereby the Greeks and the Romans managed to emphasize the text written in stone, and give an architectural status. No clever, calculated symmetrical arrangements of shapes, and no letters of different caliber, or capitals used to emphasize proper names or important words. All the signs are of the same size, one after the other, with their slender, angular shapes, their long tails and their strokes leaning this way or that. The lines are not always straight, while their limits are none other than the surface being written on. It can never have occurred to these scribes that inscriptions could be beautiful even to the eye of a person who could not understand what they said: their only aim was to carve correctly in stone a message which would be legible and clearly understood. In its script as in its system of colonisation, in its industry as in its art, the Phoenician genius had only the immediate, practical result in mind.

Carthaginian figure. Right: engravings on maritime themes, based on ancient bas-reliefs.

8 A world of merchants

In fact, it is scarcely possible to say that Phoenicia had an art at all, in the real sense of the term. It created no architectural type of its own, and did not produce any representation or rendering of living forms which was peculiar to Phoenicia alone. Its architecture and its sculpture are positively riddled with imitations and reminiscences. Rather like the unstable chemical compounds, Phoenician art readily breaks down into its component parts, which can be easily recognized as Egyptian, Chaldaean, Assyrian or, in the case of the later monuments, even Greek. When all the borrowed elements have been identified and separated, virtually nothing is left at the bottom of the jar, so to speak; indeed, the only thing which Phoenicia can truly claim as its own is the formula and the title of the mixture.

Once one enters the sphere of industry, the results are no longer the same, as this was where Phoenicia truly excelled. It showed a kind of energy, resourcefulness and sheer power that compel one's admiration. It is true that, more often than not, in ceramics, jewelry, glasswork and precious metals, it applied processes discovered by its pre-

123

decessors; but it developed them and raised them to higher levels than had ever been achieved before. In other instances, as for example, the use of purple dyes, it broke entirely new ground, and was certainly the inventor of this branch of industry, which brought it such vast profits.

Though the Phoenician genius was unsure of itself and lackluster in the field of art, nothing deterred or intimidated it when it came to travelling to remote regions looking for raw materials to be processed, or manufactured products which could be marketed at a profit. Opening up new markets and amassing a huge clientèle was quite effortless for the Phoenicians. As soon as it became likely that profits were to be made somewhere else, the Phoenician merchant would get up and go.

They visited the tribes of the Syrian deserts in order to buy the fine wool of their flocks, which was eagerly awaited, on the coast, by weavers, carders, dyers and fullers. Across both waterless wastes of sand and the dangerous fords of rain-swollen rivers, they accompanied the caravans as far as the oases of the Arabian peninsula and the gates of the cities on the Euphrates and the Tigris, as far as the foothills of the mountains of Armenia. They settled, sometimes for a few years, sometimes for a whole lifetime, at Niniveh, Babylon or Memphis, where, in the bazaar, they would have their cool, vaulted stall, where people would gather to watch the merchant fashion items of furniture or toiletries with his own hands, if he was himself a craftsman, or see the display of such goods as had been sent to him by his associates, if he was a salesman.

Many such dealers—in fact the majority—used to put to sea with their merchandise which they then offered for sale on the sands of the nearest ports along the coast; anything left over would be taken further until sold, the holds of their vessels being replenished all the time with goods from the areas visited; they kept going until the original cargo taken on board in Syria had been entirely replaced by a load of exotic goods collected along the way.

When they set sail they were carrying vases of earthenware and metal, glassware, amulets and jewels, whereas they brought back home with them animal-hides, ostrich eggs and feathers, or salmon of lead, copper and tin, depending on

whether their travels had taken them to the hot shores of Africa or the misty seas of the north, along the landmass inhabited by the Celts. On their way back they would stop over several times, depositing and collecting something at each of the trading posts where they stopped for a rest and for supplies, through their contacts with each of the barbarous tribes along their route. When they were caught away from home by the winter, they used to wait until the spring weather had come to smooth out the waves for their return passage; more than one of them, having left home a young man, only returned when his beard was turning gray with age.

The Phoenicians have left us nothing more than some epigraphic texts, which are so brief and terse that it is impossible to find in them the kind of clear view of the past, the kind of hallucination so dear to historians. When we try to bring the men of Tyr and Sidon back to life and imagine the way they were during the seven or eight centuries of their mastery of the Mediterranean, we have to turn to the Greeks, to Homer and Herodotus, in order to fill in the colors and contours of the pictures; it is through these authors that we can discover how necessary the sailors and merchants of Phoenicia had become to the semi-savage tribes of the Europe of that time, and, at the same time, how little they cared about winning the esteem or the sympathy of the people they dealt with. Their customers looked forward eagerly to their arrival, as they always came laden with glittering or useful things, but they also feared their ability to drive a hard bargain, their perfidy and their misdeeds. It was well known that, whether by ruse or by force, they took anything which was not sold to them, that they were engaged in the slave trade, and that they stopped at nothing in order to take a beautiful girl or a child with them, by fair means or foul. They were indispensable, but at the same time feared and hated. They were known as the "crafty ones", those "who knew how to cheat", those "who exploited and devoured" and who "brought a host of ills to men" (Homer).

Of all the accounts of Phoenician dealings with the Greeks, Eumea's description of the kidnapping of her nurse is so authentic and so illuminating that we have decided to reproduce it here:

126

Two views of the Phoenician ruins of the city of Motya, near Trapani, in Sicily.

"The father of Eumea, Ctesios, was the most notable citizen of Syros, an island which, despite its small size, managed to feed its cattle and sheep, had vineyards, wheatfields and two towns. The king's house was tall; in it there was a large room for the women, several outer structures, and, in front, a sort of peristyle with tables, where Ctesios used to sit and have a drink with the main citizens of the town. It was here that they discussed matters, before going to meetings of the people.

One day, some Phoenicians arrived at Syros, in black ships. Eumea greeted them in the usual manner. They had brought with them a shipload of trinkets and baubles. Ctesios had a slave from Sidon who had been sold to him by the Taphians; while washing her clothes by the river, this woman got to know her compatriots, who suggested that they should take her back home to her rich father, Arybantus. The plan was not an easy one; it was agreed that the Phoenicians would not allow it to be seen that they had noticed the servant girl, but that they would notify her on the day of their departure. The stayed a year on Syros, selling bracelets, necklaces

Left: Carthaginian gold coin (diameter: one inch).—Above: reproductions of coins from Byblos and Carthage.

129

and rings, in exchange for a type of goods which Homer does not specify; in all probability they were foodstuffs, like wheat, wine, as well as hides, and whatever else the island produced: the ship was loaded down to the gunwales with such produce.

When the time came to depart, they sent a messenger to the girl; the crafty individual offered Ctesios a gold and amber necklace, and, while the women of the household were examining it and discussing the price, the merchant made a sign to the girl that she was to go to the ship. She left with the young Eumeus, taking with her a few goblets, and, several hours later, the Phoenicians had disappeared. Six days later, the nurse was lost at sea in an accident; when the sailors landed at Ithaca they sold the young Eumeus."

This incident was fairly typical of the way the Phoenicians did business. It was a slow, leisurely process, consisting mainly of exchanging manufactured goods for natural products. In the context of the period, this sort of commerce was not so very extraordinary: all deals were done in public with no impediments, while the kidnapping of women and children were merely incidents, of no

great importance according to the customs of the day. The Phoenicians who kidnapped the young Eumeus had lived unimpeded on the island of Syros for a whole year; they must have passed the peristyle, where Ctesios and his associates used to sit drinking, more than once. Neither the people nor the king forced them to put to sea again. Of course, the crew which committed this act would not have dared show its face again in Syros for a very long time, though it is quite possible that, the next year, other Phoenicians might have put in there without being driven out by an irate mob, such was the need felt throughout the area for Phoenician merchandise and business. Indeed, the inhabitants must have regarded it as a welcome and well-merited warning to keep a closer watch over their young.

The story told by Herodotus, on the first page of his history, though much less descriptive and much shorter, about the kidnapping of Io, gives the same impression: "As soon as they had settled into the new country where they now live today, the Phoenicians went off on long sea voyages, shipping goods from Assyria and Egypt to a number of places, including Argos. In those

130

days, this city was unrivalled among all the cities of what we now know as Greece. When they landed, the Phoenicians promptly set about selling their merchandise. Five or six days after their arrival, when their sales were almost concluded, a large number of women went down to the harbor, among them Io, daughter of King Inachos. While these women were standing near the quarter deck, buying whatever came to their fancy, the Phoenicians, at an agreed signal, pounced on them, seizing Io and some others. Most of them had managed to flee. The Phoenicians then tossed them into the boat and set sail for Egypt."

The texts of Herodotus and Homer concur; they also show the kind of bitter memories left by these acts of brigandage which the Phoenicians committed without the slightest scruples, during their operations, whenever they thought they could get away with it. Here the display of goods for sale lasted only five or six days, and not a whole year, as was the case on Syros. The precise duration depended on circumstances such as the season in which the sale had begun. But the procedure was everywhere the same: the goods are laid out, as in a market, on the sand

next to the ship. Herodotus adds a comment of some interest: the Phoenician dealers offered the inhabitants of Argos, who had come rushing down on hearing of their arrival, "Assyrian and Egyptian goods". One could guess as much from the contents of the burial places of Phoenicia, Cyprus and Sardinia. During his long travels around the Mediterranean, Herodotus must have witnessed the unpacking of many a load of merchandise from Phoenician vessels.

It is easy to appreciate the sentiments of the contemporaries of Homer towards these greedy, wily dealers who, not content with abusing their monopoly by asking very high prices, occasionally acted like pirates, seizing women and children and taking them away to sea with them. Unless one is careful, one could easily espouse such rancor one's self, especially as the Phoenicians do not seem to have had at first sight, any of the brilliant qualities which can sometimes offset many a flaw. They have left mankind no beautiful poems to delight the imagination, no great buildings whose mass or fine proportions might impress the eye, and no statues embodying the purest and noblest

131

principles of art.

Nonetheless, a long, indeed almost intimate acquaintance with them shows them to us in a new, more interesting light; they were extraordinarily active, industrious, and even, in their own way, so brave and contemptuous of fatigue, danger and death! For these qualities, one might almost call them virtues, they are deserving of our esteem and gratitude. Why is it, then, that the Greeks and the Romans, who owed so much to them, never had a kind word for them? Why does the modern historian, despite his breadth of vision and his impartiality, find it a strain to be well disposed towards them?

It was because, first of all, their contemporaries of the Aryan race, the peoples of Greece and Italy, despite the daily relations which existed between them, never really got to know them and never learned their language; and, curiously enough, even we, with the efforts of modern scholarship to collect every trace, however tiny, of their script and their thinking, cannot be said to know them very much better. Moreover, there was a permanent barrier between the Greeks and Romans, on the one hand, and the Phoeni-

cians and Carthaginians, on the other. Though they traded with each other and fought each other, they never succeeded in concluding a lasting and cordial peace, and a deep mutual understanding. The two groups really remained ignorant of each other right till the end, despite a great deal of mutual borrowing; and for that reason they always remained separated by hostile sentiments and persistent antipathy.

Later on, when the races appeared to have merged into some sort of unity under the Roman Empire, the same antagonism manifested itself, only in other ways and under other conditions. It was a Semitic people, the Hebrews, who were giving the world a new religion, Christianity, and imposing on it their own literature, the Bible; yet, a short while after that religion had become so dominant, and the Hebrew books had become the sacred texts of the entire Western world, lo and behold the West began once again to persecute and to hate the Jews. Ever since their first encounter, there had been, between the two ethnic groups, much fruitful communication and, at the same time, a profound misunderstanding which has filled so many pages of history.

The Phoenicians are somewhat to blame if, still today, we find it so difficult to react against these prejudices, and to recognize and proclaim the reasons why mankind owes them such a debt of respect and gratitude. Neither the truth nor beauty impassioned them; in fact, the only passion they are known to have had is profit, and they were able to satisfy their ambitions in this direction quite amply, thanks to the particular state of the world when they entered upon the scene. In the barter trade between the barbarians and the civilized which they pursued for several centuries, the advantage was—or appeared to be—on the side of the civilized. They alone were in a position to supply certain articles, and were thus able to dictate the market conditions. This was a privilege which they both used and abused; Tyr and Carthage both amassed prodigious wealth by such means. As it happens, it is natural to feel less than indulgent, and perhaps even less than fair, towards men and nations which have become rich. Even when one has oneself benefited from them, one is inclined to argue that they have already been adequately paid for their trouble in the

135

form of the profits which they have obtained in return, and one is inclined to forget the contribution made by their good offices and their achievements. This is exactly what happened to the Phoenicians: their mind was turned excessively towards the utilitarian. They showed their concern for their own interest a little too openly, to their own disadvantage. Everyone felt entitled to be ungrateful.

It has been claimed that, if the Phoenicians did help the other peoples emerge from barbarity and develop their own genius to the full, they were unaware of it at the time, or gave such help grudgingly. This may be so, but this consideration in no way detracts from the accomplishments which can be attributed to them. Phoenicia had appropriated all the equipment and the know-how of the ancient eastern civilizations, and, through numerous ingenious improvements, particularly the invention of script, they enhanced the value of that ancient treasure even further. Whether or not they intended or were even aware of it, the Phoenicians inexorably found themselves distributing the secret of such valuable knowledge to the tribes of the is-

lands and of Europe who were then ignorant of civilized ways. The fact is that, even if the possessors of such knowledge had tried to keep it to themselves, these tribes, given a minimum of intelligence and curiosity on their part, would have been able to pry it out of them. As soon as the oar and the sail joined hitherto remote shores, the transfer of such information was inevitable. It happens that the Phoenicians were the first to land on the shores where the ancestors of Athens and Rome were still in the Stone Age.

We have mentioned the jealous zeal with which the Phoenicians sought to keep—at the cost of lies and even murder—their secret knowledge of the routes which led to the markets of the Syrtes, the coasts of Sardinia and Spain, and, further away again, to the great ocean, and the remote country from which tin could be obtained. But, despite all their precautions, the daring journeys undertaken by the Phoenicians who were much bolder navigators than the Greeks, did much to broaden and rectify the notion of the world, which, in ancient Greece, was still so narrow and inaccurate. Homer, who wrote towards the 10th century, is a case in point. Thanks to

136

their endeavors, the limits of what the Greeks called the "inhabited earth" were gradually pushed back. The human mind conceived more accurately the scope of the domain which was being opened up to its enterprise, and the vast areas which it was called upon to populate and develop; it achieved a better understanding of the mortal destiny of the human being, and the variety of relations which could exist between it and the different environments in which it was to live and grow.

Though driven by different motives, and acting in different circumstances, the sailors of Tyr and Carthage, the Hannon, the Himilcon, and so many others today forgotten, played the same sort of role in the cramped Mediterranean basin and the threshold of the Atlantic as was to be played centuries later by the great explorers who discovered the New World and the Far East. The same perseverance, the same fearlessness and the same dangers, yet without the intoxicating excitement of the battlefield. In both cases, the same effects were achieved: primitive tribes were joined to the community of civilized nations by bonds which would never be broken again. These peoples were

thus enabled to equal, and if their own native genius qualified them for it, to surpass within a short while, their more advanced rivals and their masters.

Many ships were wrecked, on dark nights, by hidden reefs, and many a sailor's life was lost before the Phoenician cities succeeded in becoming the warehouse of the entire world, and before they managed to set up a regular flow of trade between nations separated by colossal distances, and sometimes unaware even of each other's names: between Celts and Arabs, Etruscans and Assyrians, between Spaniards and Indians.

138

These results are all the more striking when one considers the meagerness of the resources with which they were attained. Even at the height of their expansion, there were never more than a few hundred thousands pure bred Phoenicians. With these small numbers they had to manage to be everywhere at once, to arrange safe havens and staging points at which their ships could be replenished, and fortified trading posts where they could store their merchandise pending its distribution to the local clientèle, and the shipment back to Tyr and Carthage of the raw materials obtained from the local markets, as soon as the fine weather returned.

It comes as something of a shock to learn that this people, which virtually lived for commerce, did not invent money; yet, when one thinks about it, nothing could be more natural. The type of business the Phoenicians were engaged in for a thousand years did not involve the use of money, and therefore did not suggest its invention. Neither Egypt nor Chaldaea, with which the Phoenicians traded from the beginning, were familiar with the minting of coins. As for all the insular and mainland tribes which they soon ventured to call upon, even if coins had been in use at the time, it would not have occurred to them to offer them to their customers, because their entire business was based on barter, which did not require, as at Memphis or Babylon, the weighing of precious metals. These tribes were as yet unaware of the arrangement whereby, in order to facilitate transactions, Egyptians and Assyrians most commonly assessed the value of the most useful everyday objects in weights of gold and silver. In their trade with these tribes, however, the Phoenicians directly exchanged the most widely different items; it was precisely this kind of deal that gave the Phoenicians their highest profits.

The alphabet is the work, and the gift, of a people of merchants which did not leave behind it one single immortal page, and which wrote more or less at the level of an bookkeeper; on the other hand, it was a people of poets and artists, the Greeks, which first issued coins, the valid and mobile representation of true worth without which trade of any sort now seems virtually impossible.

Left: funeral mask, gold, from the first millenium BC (Louvre).

139

9　A decisive step for mankind

Even if the Phoenicians had made no other contribution besides the alphabet, this would still have been a justification for their glory. For their part, they took only minimal advantage of it, but they did transmit it to all the peoples with which they did business: for them, the alphabet was an export item. They always charged a fat commission on anything they supplied to their Greek or Italian clients. They rejoiced at the ease with which they had fooled the immature tribes which were henceforth dependent on trade with them; however, in the long run, it seems that the greatest profit was realized by those who often thought they were on the losing end of the deal.

The Phoenicians sold their goods for more than they were worth; yet, when they sailed off, content with their deviousness, they nonetheless left behind them the alphabet with which the Greeks later created philosophy, history and science; they left figurines of bronze, ivory, enamelled earthenware or stone, clay or metal vases, painted or carved, which suggested the idea of certain divine types and aroused a feeling for shape among a people whose sculptors were to be Phidias and Praxiteles. The nascent industries of the tribes with whom they traded were likewise helped by the presence of materials, models and tools all left by the Phoenicians.

The Phoenicians were quintessentially men of all trades. Many of them, before going to sea, had worked in a craftsman's shop, and could repair tools damaged during the voyage, make a vase, and patch together a weapon or a jewel. While the merchant was busy working, a crowd would gather around him; a casual glance was all that was needed to discover the secret of the composition of a soldering fluid, or to grasp the knack of this or that operation.

When one tries to visualize what happened whenever a Phoenician ship put into shore, or to calculate the useful effect of all these contacts and exchanges of products and ideas, one cannot fail to feel a measure of sympathy towards these remarkable men, as the Sidonian galley put out to sea, with neither chart nor compass. To begin with, the ship would hug the coast timidly, hastening into the nearest cove at the first sign of bad weather; then it would wait for the wind to drop, after which the captain would venture out, emboldened, across a stretch of

A group of Phoenician tombs at Utica, Tunisia.

141

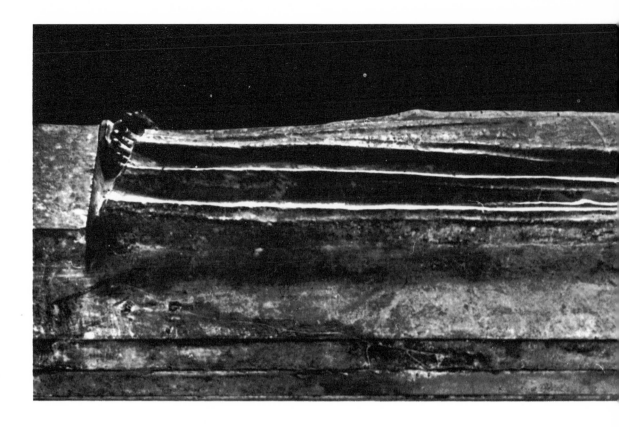

open water to an island such as Cyprus or Rhodes, whose distant mountains could be seen on the horizon. On arrival there, the crew would rest, and then venture on another, longer crossing, out of sight of land. The vessel might be swept away by the storm towards the inhospitable Syrtes, or it might fight its way across the rough Adriatic. We would probably applaud when, after weathering more than one storm, it finally reached a safe haven on the coast of Italy or Sicily, following a route unknown to others.

Standing with the sailors on the sand, we would enthusiastically join in the prayers and giving of thanks to the great god of Phoenicia, Melqart, who had guided them and saved them during their dangerous and anxious crossing.

Unlike his Greek successor, Heracles, the Phoenician Melqart, to whom we cannot even attach a face or any features, was never transfigured in art or poetry; he was not born out of Zeus in the morning light, later to die on Ossa, in the splendor of the setting sun, rise into

142

Greco-Phoenician sarcophagus at Carthage (most probably that of a priest).

heaven and become the spouse of Hebe, the immortal goddess of youth; yet he certainly earned the incense which burnt on his altars, and the victims whose blood poured over them. How many ships sailed the seas, confident of his protection, and how many lands were then opened to trade by the Christopher Columbus's of the Mediterranean! Without the Melqart of Tyr, without the sailors he guided across the unknown, how sadly the thrust of civilization would have been restrained, and how severely its movement al-

tered! Who can say how long the ancestors of the Greeks and Romans would have remained in the primitive state which was common to various European tribes up to the beginning of the Christian era! The heroic effort represented by Phoenician navigation and colonisation enabled mankind to make a remarkable, indeed, a decisive, leap forward.